Moonscapes

A Celebration of Lunar Astronomy, Magic, Legend and Lore

by Rosemary Ellen Guiley

PRENTICE
HALL
PRESS

New York   London   Toronto   Sydney   Tokyo   Singapore

DEDICATION

In memory of J. Donald Guiley
ad astra

ACKNOWLEDGMENTS

My deepest thanks to Margaret L. Guiley for assisting me with the research for this book, and
to Bruce S. Trachtenberg for his invaluable help in putting all the pieces together.

PRENTICE HALL PRESS
15 Columbus Circle
New York, NY   10023

Library of Congress Cataloging-in-Publication Data

Guiley, Rosemary.
    Moonscapes : a celebration of lunar astronomy, magic, legend, and
lore / Rosemary Ellen Guiley.
        p. cm.
    Includes index.
    ISBN 0-13-541681-7 : $17.95
    1. Moon—Popular works.   2. Moon—Mythology.   I. Title.
QB581.9.G85   1991
523.3—dc20   90-27699
                                                                              CIP

Produced by Cynthia Parzych Publishing Inc.
Designed by Peter Helinski
Edited by Jean Hoots

Typeset by Pagesetters, Inc.
Printed and bound by Ocean Graphic Printing, Inc. in Hong Kong

First Prentice Hall Press Edition 1991

Contents

Preface **4**

Introduction **6**

The Peculiar Nature of the Moon **7**

Moon Myths and Other Tales **43**

Moon Rites and Mysteries **75**

Rhythms of Life **99**

Moon Magic **115**

Moon Madness and Night Things **141**

Man on the Moon and Beyond **161**

Bibliography **190**

Photo Credits **191**

Index **192**

Preface

When I was six years old, I got my first telescope. It wasn't much—a little black hand-held tube with low-power lenses that cost my parents fifty cents and a box top from Kix cereal. But to me it was a magical instrument, for it magnified the objects in the heavens. The first thing I turned it on was the moon. Night after night, I stood in our backyard in Seattle, Washington, gazing at the moon, in awe of what I saw through that little black tube. My friend and neighbor, Mary Rice, would join me, and we took turns examining the moon, the stars and the planets. We were too young to know it then, but we were swept up in a mystery that has moved the human race since the dawn of its history. What is it up there, that shining, silvery world? Where did it come from, and what does it mean to us?

That little telescope and my early moon-gazing led to an active interest in amateur astronomy that engaged my father, J. Donald Guiley, as well. Together we spent many years charting the skies. We built our own telescope (an eight-inch reflector), we photographed the moon and other celestial objects, we observed eclipses and occultations, we watched meteor showers, we kept voluminous records. We became officers in the Seattle Astronomical Society (SAS). In particular, Dad enjoyed working with young people, and he had an enthusiastic following in the junior division of the SAS. He also worked as a volunteer for the Seattle School District, bringing the wonders of the heavens into the classroom.

Eventually, my father's outstanding contributions to amateur astronomy in the northwest region were recognized. An observatory built by the Tacoma Astronomical Society in Puyallup, Washington, was named the Pettinger-Guiley Observatory, and dedicated on August 11, 1979. Dad shared the honors with a Tacoma colleague, Norm Pettinger, a founding member of the Tacoma Astronomical Society. The observatory was built by amateur astronomer Al George with the help of the Tacoma Astronomical Society. It was Al's childhood dream to have his own observatory, and the facility he now owns serves a large community of amateur astronomers, as well as visitors from afar, and offers programs to the public. The Tacoma Astronomical Society assists in all the activities.

Initially, the observatory housed a six-inch refractor telescope. This was replaced by an eight-inch refractor, then a ten-inch refractor. In January 1991, the observatory installed the fifteen-inch Swanson refractor, the largest refractor telescope in the northwestern United States. The telescope is named after Al Swanson, a fellow amateur astronomer who built in his own workshop much of the observatory's equipment, including the steel pier and mounting for the Swanson refractor.

It's deeply fulfilling to see my father's name live on in the field that he loved so much. I have never lost my own interest in astronomy, or my wonder at the heavens. In later years I became intrigued, in addition to scientific inquiry, with moon lore—the wealth of myth, legend, folklore and superstition surrounding the moon. No other celestial object has excited such interest over the millennia. This book presents a collection of moon lore and science gems and nuggets intended to stir our ancient and collective longing to understand the earth's companion, the moon.

— Rosemary Ellen Guiley, 1991

Introduction

The contents of this book are arranged to take you on a journey. We begin with "The Peculiar Nature of the Moon," an overview of history and science.

"Moon Myths and Other Tales" explains humankind's earliest efforts, through myths and legends, to comprehend the moon, its origins and nature.

"Moon Rites and Mysteries" tells how various civilizations have sought the moon's favor through worship of deities. Mighty lunar gods and goddesses were (and still are in some parts of the world) the keys to the moon's time-keeping and its perceived power to regulate life and bestow magical power.

From the sacred we move to the mundane. "Rhythms of Life" discusses how the earlier myths and beliefs became codified into bodies of folklore concerning the moon's influence on gardening, farming, weather, folk remedies, love and marriage, illness, personal hygiene and medicine.

Magic is one way humankind attempts to change circumstances and manipulate the forces and powers of nature. In "Moon Magic" you'll find out how magical spells call on the moon. The chapter features the moon's role in ceremonial magic, and in astrology, scrying, palmistry and the Tarot.

We peek into the dark side in "Moon Madness and Night Things" to consider whether the moon influences insanity, moods and crime. The supernatural world of werewolves, vampires and other strange creatures of the night is also examined.

Finally, "Man on the Moon and Beyond" describes the history of unmanned and manned space flights to the moon, and chronicles the adventures of the American astronauts who flew there and returned. We end our own journey considering the future. Inevitably, we will return to the moon and someday build colonies there.

No matter how much we observe, measure, ponder and explore, the moon may never yield all her secrets to us. She is likely to remain forever remote and enigmatic, as mysterious today and tomorrow as she was thousands of years ago.

The Peculiar Nature of the Moon

To early humankind, the moon was the land of gods and a repository of the souls of the dead. It played center stage in myths that explained the creation of the universe. It worked magic on the earth and on all living things under its cold light. Mysteriously, the tides rose and fell in rhythm with the moon. Unlike the sun, steady and constant in the sky, the moon was changeable, growing and diminishing in size, and yet it always looked upon the earth with the same enigmatic face.

Early astronomers studied the moon and attempted to explain its features and nature, but they were limited to what they could observe with the naked eye. Ptolemy, the second-century Greco-Egyptian astronomer, explained the planetary movements in terms of an earth-centered universe. He saw the moon as occupying the first orbit around the earth, followed by the sun and other planets visible to the naked eye. Ptolemy was right in determining that the moon revolves around the earth

and is the closest planetary body, but wrong about the sun and planets circling the earth. Nonetheless, his system was the accepted belief until the Polish astronomer Nicolaus Copernicus (1473–1543) blew it apart with a sun-centered model. The Church called it heresy, but the Copernican theory eventually proved itself.

Some early observers thought the moon was flat because they could discern no shadings around its edges. The truth is, nearly all the full moon's surface is equally illuminated because of its unusual texture.

The first known map of the moon was drawn around 1600 by William Gilbert, physician to Queen Elizabeth I. Gilbert believed the dark areas to be land and the bright areas to be seas, contrary to later thought.

The invention of the telescope in 1608 enabled scientists to probe the lunar mysteries with more skill. Galileo Galilei (1564–1642) was the first to use an "optik tube," which had a magnify-

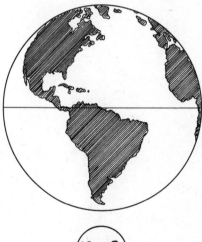

Relative sizes of the earth and moon drawn to scale.

ing power of thirty times. It was sufficient to reveal craters, mountains and huge, dark, plainlike areas. Galileo made a rough map of the moon and attempted to measure the height of its mountains. Much of his mapping was inaccurate, although he was uncannily accurate in estimating the peaks as up to five miles in height.

Another astronomer of the day, Giambattista Riccioli (1598–1671), named the craters after great scientists and philosophers. He also named dark areas *maria*, Latin for "seas," in the belief that they were seas or dried sea-beds, and gave them each poetic names, such as the Sea of Tranquility, the Foaming Sea and the Sea of Fertility. The names remain today, though the *maria* were recognized as plains, not seas, by one of Riccioli's contemporaries, Johan Hewelcke, or Hevelius (1611–1687).

Scientific knowledge advanced through the centuries, aided by the advent of astrophotography around the turn of the twentieth century and culminating in the manned Apollo moon missions of the 1960s and 1970s, when humans were able to observe the moon

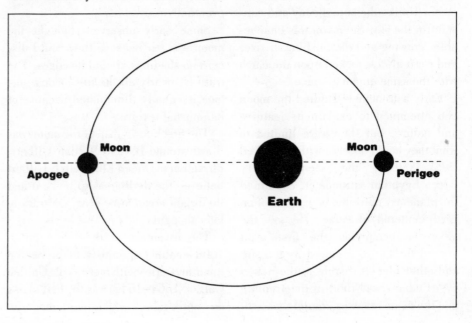

The moon orbits the earth in an ellipse, reaching its closest point at perigee and its farthest point at apogee.

while standing on its surface and to collect pieces of it to bring back to earth for analysis. We may not make more significant advances in our understanding of the moon until we establish a colony on the moon and live there.

The Moon's Orbit

With a diameter of 2,160 miles (3,476 kilometers), the moon measures just 27 percent the size of the earth. It orbits the earth in an ellipse, not a circle, at an average speed of 2,287 miles (3,680 kilometers) per hour. The time it takes for a complete journey around the earth, with respect to a fixed star, is 27 days, 7 hours, 43 minutes and 11.5 seconds—a sidereal month or sidereal period. The cycle from new moon to new moon lasts 29.53 days and is called the lunation or synodic month.

The moon speeds up to about 2,429 miles (3,908 kilometers) per hour when it is at perigee, the closest point in its orbit to the earth, and slows to about 2,153 miles (3,464 kilometers) per hour when it is at apogee, the farthest point.

As the moon spins around us, it rotates slowly on its own axis, making one complete spin every 27.32 days. The combined revolution and rotation pe-

riods cause the moon to present the same face to us all the time. The calendar we use, called the Gregorian calendar, is not a lunar one. A true lunar month is slightly shorter than the Gregorian calendar month, and so there is a "slippage," called retardation, averaging about 50 minutes a day in the rising and setting of the moon. The retardation varies. For example, it is only about 20 minutes in September, which allows the full moon to be seen in the early evening for several nights in a row—hence, the Harvest Moon, whose light gives farmers a longer time to gather crops.

The Lunar Surface

The moon is virtually airless and devoid of water. It has no light of its own, but reflects sunlight. It appears to be a colorless, still world, yet colors and unusual active phenomena have been observed on its surface.

Even a small telescope will reveal the staggering majesty of the moon: sweeping plains, thrusting peaks, deep valleys and assorted markings. Scientists have given these formations specific classifications, including: *maria*, or seas (the plains); *paludes*, or marshes, similar to but smaller than the

The lunar surface as a nineteenth century artist imagined it might look.

9

The Ten Largest Craters on The Moon

Crater	Diameters	Location
Bailly	184 miles/296 km.	southeast
Clavius	140 miles/225 km.	southwest
Schickard	139 miles/224 km.	southwest
Humboldt	130 miles/209 km.	southeast
Grimaldi	138 miles/222 km.	southwest
Maginus	101 miles/163 km.	southwest
Schiller	112 miles/180 km.	southwest
Petavius	110 miles/177 km.	southwest
Riccioli	94 miles/151 km.	southwest
Hipparchus	93 miles/150 km.	southwest

(Looking with the naked eye, or through binoculars, north is at top, west is at left. Through a telescope, north and south are inverted, south being at the top.)

Craters and rilles viewed from Apollo 15 in orbit.

seas; *sinii*, or bays and gulfs; bright plains; mountain ranges; isolated hills; uplands and peaks; *rilles*, or deep trenches or clefts; valleys and gorges; bright rays; bright areas; and ringed structures. The ringed structures are further divided into walled plains, mountain rings, ringed plains, crater plains, craters, craterlets, cratercones, craterpits, obscure rings and depressions.

Much of the lunar surface is pockmarked with craters. The smallest are tiny depressions, while the largest measure up to 184 miles (296 kilometers) in diameter. Many overlap, and some have a peak or several peaks in the center. The largest craters and many small ones were probably formed by meteor impact—the moon has no atmosphere to burn up meteors, as does the earth—while others may have been formed by ancient, now defunct, volcanic activity.

The *maria*, which never bore water, were at one time huge lava flows that solidified into basalt. Few craters exist on them. Many of the seas are circular, with portions of their perimeters bounded by chains of Alpine-like mountains scaling up to 20,000 feet (6,096 meters) or more in height. Running parallel to mountain chains are *rilles*, trenches up to about 184 miles

(296 meters) in length that sometimes cut through crater walls. There are more than 2,000 known *rilles*; whole systems of them snake over the moon's surface. Some of them are not actually trenches, but chains of overlapping craters.

The moon's isolated peaks are rarely over 8,000 feet (2,438 kilometers) in height, but nonetheless are impressive to behold. Most of them are in the area of the moon called the bright uplands. In the same area are numerous domes, swellings of the surface that may have been the result of internal pressure that blistered but never broke the surface.

Perhaps the most spectacular feature to the casual observer is the system of bright white rays emanating like giant spokes from certain craters. The rays are best seen at full moon. The largest and most brilliant surround the craters Tycho and Copernicus. From Tycho, a modestly sized crater 54 miles (87 kilometers) in diameter, hundreds of rays stretch out, spanning a diameter of up to 1,900 miles (3,057 kilometers).

None of the rays penetrate the craters they surround; there is a dark "free zone" between craters and the beginnings of the rays. Most rays are peppered with small craters and craterlets.

Little is known about the rays, de-

Lunar Seas	
Latin Name	**English Name**
Sinus Aestuum	Bay of Heats
Mare Australe	Southern Sea
Mare Crisium	Sea of Crises
Palus Epidemiarum	Marsh of Epidemics
Mare Fecunditatis	Sea of Fertility
Mare Frigoris	Sea of Cold
Mare Humboldtinaum	Humboldt's Sea
Mare Humorum	Sea of Humours
Mare Imbrium	Sea of Showers
Sinus Iridum	Bay of Rainbows
Mare Marginis	Marginal Sea
Sinus Medii	Central Bay
Lacus Mortis	Lake of Death
Palus Nebularum	Marsh of Mists
Mare Nectaris	Sea of Nectar
Mare Nubium	Sea of Clouds
Mare Orientale	Eastern Sea
Oceanus Procellarum	Ocean of Storms
Palus Putredinis	Marsh of Decay
Sinus Roris	Bay of Dews
Mare Serenitatis	Sea of Serenity
Mare Smythii	Smyth's Sea
Palus Somnii	Marsh of Sleep
Lacus Somniorum	Lake of Dreamers
Mare Spumans	Foaming Sea
Mare Tranquillitatis	Sea of Tranquility
Mare Undarum	Sea of Waves

Dark areas are vast plains once believed to be seas, or *maria*.

spite the fact that Apollo astronauts have visited them. They appear to be thin surface deposits associated with bright, young craters. In January 1968, the unmanned probe Surveyor 7 landed

Rays streaming from several craters light up lunar landscape.

The Great Ray Craters

Crater	Diameters	Ray Diameters	Location
Aristillus	35 miles/ 56 km.	400 miles/ 644 km.	northwest
Copernicus	57 miles/ 92 km.	750 miles/1,207 km.	northwest
Kepler	20 miles/ 32 km.	400 miles/ 644 km.	northwest
Langrenus	82 miles/132 km.	950 miles/1,529 km.	southeast
Olbers	42 miles/ 68 km.	500 miles/ 805 km.	northwest
Strabo	34 miles/ 55 km.	400 miles/ 644 km.	northeast
Theophilus	64 miles/103 km.	675 miles/1,086 km.	southeast
Tycho	54 miles/ 87 km.	1,900 miles/3,057 km.	southwest

"Canals" On The Moon

At the turn of the twentieth century, lines were observed crisscrossing the surface of Mars. The American astronomer Percival Lowell (1855–1916) believed the lines to be artificial irrigation canals, thus fueling intense controversy and debate over the possible existence of life on the planet. In the wake of the Mariner and Viking space probes, we know that Mars has no irrigation canals, though there are natural channels which may have held water but long ago went dry.

At about the same time, an almost exact counterpart to the Martian "canals" was observed on the moon both with the naked eye and through a telescope. The lunar "canals" were first noted in 1896 by Signor Cerulli, and some fifty of them were mapped within twenty years.

Alas, the lunar "canals" proved to be illusions. When telescopes with greater magnifying power were turned on the lines, many disappeared. They were anomalies created by the tendency of the eye and brain to combine diverse markings into well-defined features—which disappear under close scrutiny.

Lineaments do exist on the moon and have been photographed by spacecraft. They appear to be fractures, faults, shear zones and what is called "stratigraphic layering."

at Tycho and found an unusual amount of aluminum present and less iron than has been found at other sites.

Scientists can only speculate how the rays were formed. Though they are intimately associated with their hub craters, they may not have been formed at the same time as the craters. Some rays blend in end-to-end with rays from other craters of different ages. Rays that approach other rays from a considerable angle end abruptly at the point of intersection. Some rays have gaps in them.

While the moon is a dead and sterile world, it is not inactive. Slow changes occur due to moonquakes and the impact of meteorites. Transient lunar phenomena (TLPs) also indicate a low level of lunar activity. TLPs include temporal points of light, apparent clouds, streaks of apparent lightning and other luminescence. It is believed that TLPs are caused by unusual reflections of sunlight and particles from the sun, incandescence of lunar gases, or phenomena in the earth's atmosphere that are made visible against a lunar backdrop.

The Birth of the Moon

While scientists are in general agreement about the creation of the solar system and the planets, the origin of the moon remains an enigma. As a modern-day scientist said, "The moon must really not exist because we can't explain it."

From 1796 to about 1900, many scientists accepted the Nebular Hypothesis, which held that the moon and planets formed from rotating and condensing gas clouds. That was disproved and replaced by three other theories.

One theory stated that the moon started out as a small body that rotated around the earth, eventually growing larger and larger with accumulated debris from space.

Another theory said that the moon spun off from the earth. Supposedly, the earth rotated so fast that it became unstable and the moon was formed when the tidal forces from the sun tore away a piece of the planet at the equator.

According to the third theory, the moon formed elsewhere in the solar system and gravitational forces pulled it into the earth's orbit.

After analyzing soil and rock samples the Apollo astronauts brought back from the moon, scientists concluded that no proof exists to support any of the three dominant theories of the moon's origins. A fourth theory emerged. It proposed that the moon was born following a cataclysmic collision between the earth and a planet about the size of Mars.

According to this theory, another astral body slammed into the earth when it was still molten. The impact was so powerful that it blew most of the earth's mantle away, leaving its iron core exposed. The explosion also spewed hot silicate gases upward into space. A cloud of hot gas and debris formed

Mosaic showing earth with sun flare rising above moon, Venus to left. Top row, l to r: Jupiter, Mercury, Mars, Saturn.

Why the Moon is Made of Green Cheese

Sayings about the moon being made of green cheese probably relate to expressions that one who is inexperienced or naive is "green," as well as to the fact that new or green cheeses resemble the moon. Writing in *Proverbs,* John Heywood stated that anyone who might "thinke that the moone is made of green cheese . . . is a dolt and a fool." Similarly, Erasmus stated in *Adagia* (1500), "He made his friends believe the moon is made of green cheese."

around the earth. This material eventually cooled, coalesced and became the moon. In the beginning, the orbit of the moon was closer to the earth than it is today. Over the next several thousand years, the moon moved outward, sweeping more and more debris into itself. Computer models demonstrate that this theory is the most likely explanation of how the moon was formed.

The Substance of the Moon

Analysis of moon soil collected by the unmanned lunar missions and of the rocks brought to earth by the Apollo astronauts reveals no unknown substances or chemical elements on the lunar surface. Just as on earth, oxygen seems to be the most prevalent element, accounting for up to 42 percent of the atomic structure of the moon. Some of the elements that occur more abundantly than on earth are aluminum, nitrogen, calcium, titanium, magnesium and ytterbium.

Structurally, too, the moon is similar to the earth. It has a crust, a mantle and a core. The crust and mantle are thicker than the earth's, a condition that could be caused if the moon's internal temperature is cooler.

The so-called lunar soil is composed mostly of surface rock broken up over billions of years of continuous bombardment by meteorites. It measures on the average 2 or 3 feet (about 75 centimeters) in depth, though at places it may be as deep as 60 feet (18 meters). It is organically dead.

The remaining surface rocks were formed from cooling lava. Although made of the same substances as earth rocks, moon rocks look different because they were formed without water.

One of the puzzling findings of the lunar missions was that the soil appears to be older than the surface rocks. How is that possible if the soil originated from the rocks? One suggestion is that the existing rocks were formed by lava flows that came after the soil was created and thus are not the original source of the soil on the moon. In other words, there were older rocks on the moon that have since become lunar soil.

Other analyses of moon rocks showed a remnant of magnetization. The moon's weak magnetic field and the presence of magnetism in the rocks suggest that the moon did have a stronger magnetic field three or four billion years ago— about one billion years after it was created.

Of all the discoveries, one of the

Shake, Rattle and Roll

Floating high above us in the night sky, the moon looks so quiet and peaceful. Who would think that there are forces at work deep beneath the surface? The fact is that "moonquakes" occur as frequently as twice daily, according to seismic monitors left on the surface of the moon by Apollo crews. Moon tremors are far less powerful than quakes on earth; they give off about as much energy as an exploding firecracker. If you were standing on the moon during a quake, you probably would not feel a thing.

Scientists believe the quakes are caused by shifts in the layers of the moon. Some quakes are relatively close to the surface—about 15 miles (24 kilometers) deep, while others occur much closer to the moon's molten core, which is about 900 miles (1,448 kilometers) deep.

Quakes are also caused by meteorites striking the moon. There is even some speculation that gravitational forces from the earth, comparable to the ocean tides, cause movement within the moon that results in quakes.

Moonquakes occur more frequently at perigee. They appear to be the cause of surface changes, such as the appearance, shifting and disappearance of cracks.

---

more interesting findings was the scarcity of dust on the moon's surface. Some scientists had speculated that astronauts would find such deep accumulations of dust, their landing craft would get mired. In reality, the total amount of dust near where the first craft landed was no more than one–eighth of an inch thick. Later missions set down in the *maria*, again looking for dust. The maximum accumulations never exceeded 3 inches (about 8 centimeters). Considering that the moon is billions of years old, the effects of ultraviolet light and solar X rays on exposed lunar rock should have produced as much as 6.3 miles (10 kilometers) of dust.

Apollo astronauts were surprised also to find glassy veneer on lunar rock. The glassy formations were later explained to be the result of violent shocks to the surface, such as heat released when a meteor struck. Another suggestion is that they were formed by an intense blast of solar radiation.

Heat and Cold

Temperatures hit a high of 273° F (134° C) during the equivalent of the lunar summer, when the moon is facing the sun. Similarly, when the moon is turned away from the sun, the surface temperature plummets to a frigid −244° F (−153° C).

The Mysterious, Unseen Far Side

For centuries, humankind yearned to know what was on the far side of the moon—the surface that cannot be seen from earth.

At last, in 1959 the Russian unmanned spacecraft Luna III traveled to the dark side and photographed the unseen face.

The Luna III photos, like those from the many moon missions since then, contained few surprises. The far side differs little from the near side. It appears to have fewer large *maria*—those great dark planes on the surface of the moon once believed to be seas, and much of the surface is more elevated than the near side. Also, based on analysis of the apparent results of meteor bombardment, scientists concluded that the crust on the far side is thicker than the near side.

There is one link between the two sides of the moon, and that is the huge Mare Orientale, which reaches around the eastern limb of the far side to the more familiar near side.

Because the moon takes about 27.32 days to complete its rotation, the lunar day and night are each equivalent to about fourteen earth days. That means the moon broils under the sun's rays for two weeks. For the remaining fourteen days, it is deprived of sunlight.

The extremely thin atmosphere on the moon provides nothing to block the direct rays of the sun and temper its heat. The airlessness also means no cooling breezes to moderate the extreme heat, and nothing to trap heat, which accounts for the sudden drop in temperature when the moon turns away from the sun.

Not all surface areas record the same highs and lows. Differing elevations, reflective conditions on the surface, and areas of shade can contribute to a variety of temperatures within the same vicinity. The temperature on the ground in a shaded area can be below freezing while a nearby section in direct sunlight can be extremely hot.

The Changing Face of the Moon

The face of the moon comes and goes each month, a process of waxing and waning known as the lunar phases. The new moon, which starts the cycle, is virtually invisible. In the days that follow, the moon reveals more and more of itself as it makes its journey around the earth. Halfway through the cycle, the moon is completely illuminated. From then on the process reverses, and the moon, now in its waning phase, grows

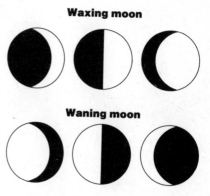

Waxing moon

Waning moon

As the moon waxes and wanes, a ragged illuminated edge slides across its face. This edge is called the terminator. The limb of the moon is the visible outer edge of the disk.

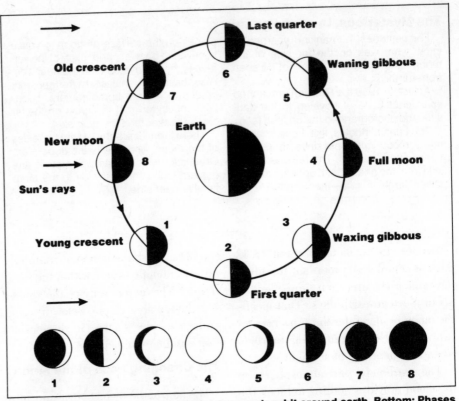

Top: The changing lunar phases relative to moon's orbit around earth. Bottom: Phases as seen from earth.

darker and darker until it disappears. At that point, the cycle begins again.

The moon disk's changing shape reflects the portion of its surface that is illuminated by the light from the sun. During its monthly cycle, the moon passes through eight phases: new moon, waxing crescent, first quarter, waxing gibbous, full moon, waning gibbous, last quarter and waning crescent.

The cycle begins when the moon is lined up directly between the sun and earth and is virtually invisible. As the moon begins to move away from the sun, the waxing crescent shape appears—a sliver of light on the right side of the moon (on our right as we face it). As the moon continues to wax, the light will grow over its surface from right to left.

By the time the moon is half lit, it has completed one-quarter of its journey around the earth, which is why it is said to be in its first quarter.

As the moon continues to grow brighter it reaches the waxing gibbous phase when it is three-quarters full. Finally, it becomes fully illuminated, or a full moon. The moon is now opposite the side of the earth from where it began as a new moon.

From this point on the moon is in its waning phase. Darkness descends from right to left. A dark crescent appears on the right side, marking the waning gibbous phase. Next comes the last quarter, when the moon is half dark. In its last phase, the only visible light is a crescent on the left side. Finally, the moon comes full circle, reaching the phase of the new moon again.

A rule of thumb to tell what phase the moon is in: when in its waxing phases, the illuminated moon grows larger from right to left. As it wanes, following the appearance of a full moon, the darkness grows from the right side.

Librations Give Us a Peek

Despite the fact the moon rotates, it never shows its far side to observers on earth. Yet, due to inconsistencies in its orbit around the earth, it is possible to get a small glance at the other side.

Librations, as the inconsistencies are called, are due to the nature of the earth's and the moon's orbits. As the moon orbits the earth, the revolution of the earth shifts our perspective 7,928 miles (12,756 kilometers) (the diameter of the earth), causing a libration in longitude. The angle between the earth's equator and the moon's orbital plane reveals otherwise unseen portions of the moon's face.

While it's never possible to see more than fifty percent of the moon's surface at any one time, thanks to librations, a total of roughly fifty-nine percent of the moon can be viewed from earth, with the other forty-one percent forever remaining hidden.

Another kind of libration causes the moon to actually wobble in its orbit. The moon does not revolve around the earth in a perfect circle but in an ellipse, which causes its distance from the earth to vary. When the moon approaches the earth, its rate of travel is faster than when it is farther. away. At

Lunar phase viewed through eight-inch reflector.

the same time, its own rotation is constant. There are times when the moon's orbit lags behind its rotation and other times when the orbit is ahead of the rotation. The moon's tidal bulge gets out of alignment with the axis of the moon and the center of the earth, and gravity attempts to realign it. This

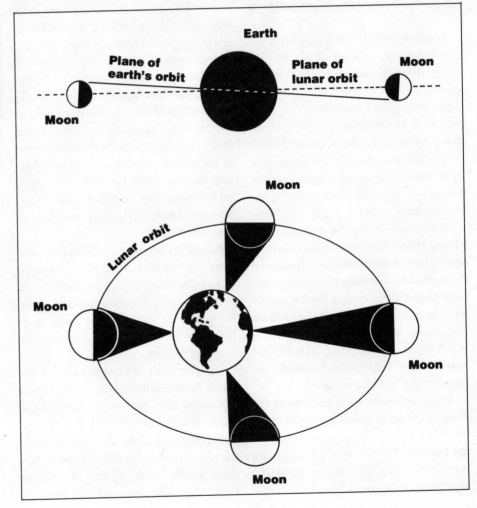

Top: A five-degree tilt in moon's orbit relative to plane of earth's orbit around sun causes latitudinal librations. Bottom: Longitudinal librations are produced by moon's elliptical orbit around earth.

causes the wobble. Scientists analyze the physical libration of the moon in order to study the moon's tidal bulges and the distribution of light and heavy materials in the moon.

Ruler of the Tides

The moon is the most important of the three gravitational forces that create tides on earth. The other two forces are the earth's own revolution and the gravitational pull from the sun.

Contrary to common belief, the moon does not create tides by directly pulling the water away from the earth as it passes above. Instead, as the moon passes away, its gravitational pull creates a bulge of water behind it. A second bulge is created on the other side of the earth as a result of the combined forces of the movement of the planet and the gravitational pull of both earth and sun. As the two bulges move around the earth, the earth itself is moving, thus affecting the movement of the tides.

These three forces also combine to create differing tidal effects at various times of the year. The highest and lowest monthly tides, called spring tides (which can occur throughout the year), result when the sun, moon and earth

are in a line and pulling in the same direction. High and low tides that hardly differ, or neap tides, occur when the sun and moon are at right angles.

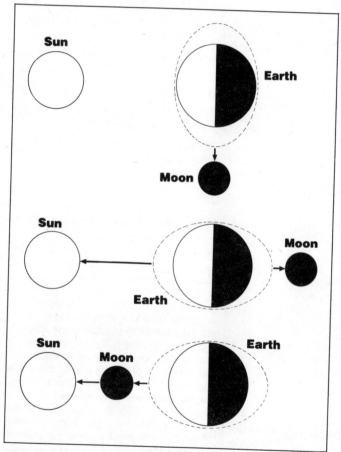

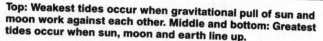
Top: Weakest tides occur when gravitational pull of sun and moon work against each other. Middle and bottom: Greatest tides occur when sun, moon and earth line up.

Mock moon

Halo

Moon pillar

Lunar zodiacal light

And the Lunar Weather Forecast Is . . .

Predicting the weather on earth is no easy task. On the moon, there is nothing to it. There is no weather to predict.

Despite the virtual lack of atmosphere and water, the usual phenomena that create weather conditions on earth—mists and clouds—have been observed on the moon. Are they gases released from beneath the surface by moonquakes? Or lunar dust stirred upwards by striking meteors? Perhaps both, but no one knows for sure. The phenomena are puzzling because the airless lunar conditions should cause clouds to disperse immediately.

Clearly, something has been happening on the moon. In 1826, the German selenographer Franz von Gruithuisen observed "a veil or mist that appeared to extend" over a portion of the surface.

Forty years later, another lunar observer reported that the crater Linné was concealed by a sort of fog or haze. When the fog cleared, the crater appeared to have been replaced by a smaller one with a white spot.

At a meeting of the Liverpool Astro-

Mock Moons and Strange Lights

When atmospheric conditions are right, unusual optical displays are seen around the moon. Such phenomena have played an important role in the weather prognostications of folklore.

A *mock moon,* also called a *moon dog,* is a pale, false image of the moon which appears just off to the side of the moon. It is produced by the refraction of moonlight in cold and moist air, but depends on certain humidity conditions and on the angle and sight of the observer. Mock moons usually occur two or three days after full phase. They often are seen in association with haloes. It is possible for as many as eight or nine mock moons to appear at the same time.

A *halo* or *moonbow* is a lunar version of a rainbow, though much less vivid. It appears as a colorful ring around the moon when the moon's light is refracted through droplets of moisture in the earth's air.

A *moon pillar* is another type of lunar halo, though very rare. It is not a complete halo, but is like shafts of light that appear above and below the moon. It occurs during certain atmospheric conditions when the moon is low on the horizon.

Lunar zodiacal light consists of cones of luminous light extending from either side of the moon along the plane of the ecliptic. It probably is caused by the reflection of moonlight on clouds of gas, particles or electrons in the earth's atmosphere. It often appears in conjunction with solar zodiacal light, a cone of faint light seen in the west shortly after sunset or in the east shortly before sunrise.

nomical Society in 1882, one member said he had "often noticed appearances which could only be accounted for by the existence of a lunar haze."

Some astronomers, when confronted by inexplicable cloud formations, refused to believe what they saw, as one observer noted in 1932. "A white spot made its appearance and in less than a minute it had spread in a northeasterly direction until it almost reached the rim of the crater. This observation was verified by my friend as I rather doubted my own eyes. It appeared and moved like a cloud of steam . . . but this idea seems untenable."

In the following account, two amateur astronomers, one with twenty years' experience, provide a detailed description of a large cloud the pair observed in 1958. "While sweeping the moon's surface, we were startled by what we saw within the crater Alphonsus. A large diffuse cloud completely obscured the crater's central mountain peak and its small craterlet. The cloud was about twenty miles in diameter and irregular in shape.

"Two main features attracted our attention: The cloud was large in comparison to the peak that it obscured and it had a strange diffuse brightness."

In addition to clouds and gases, lightning has been seen on the moon more than once. In 1931, a government scientist and his wife, who had been working in their back yard in Riverside, California, were startled by what they saw when they looked up at the new moon one evening. "Flashes of light streaked across the dark surface but definitely within the limits of the moon's outline," recorded the scientist. "A minute or two later, I saw similar flashes streak across the moon. I asked my wife if she had noticed anything strange. She said, 'Oh, yes, I see lightning on the moon.' "

Scientists suggest that lunar lightning may be some sort of flashing light in the outer atmosphere of the earth that is made more visible against the backdrop of the moon.

When the Sun and Moon Are Eaten

To primitive peoples, the two most important celestial objects, the sun and the moon, fostered and regulated all life on earth. If anything occurred to threaten the existence or function of these two bodies, chaos and catastrophe would surely follow. Perhaps the world would come to an end.

Imagine the uproar that must have occurred whenever the sun and moon diminished in light or seemed to disappear from the sky or become covered with blood—for that is what seems to happen during an eclipse.

There are two kinds of eclipses, lunar and solar, and the moon plays a key role in both. Lunar eclipses are the more common of the two. For those fortunate enough to see them, solar eclipses are the more awesome spectacle. In a solar eclipse, the sun seems to disappear from the heavens. Sometimes it completely vanishes, while at other times just a bright ring flashes in the sky.

Lunar eclipses have their magical ef-

Eclipse Anomalies

Some observers have recorded what can only be called eclipse anomalies.

In a very dark lunar eclipse, the moon completely vanishes from view and can barely be seen through a telescope. This type of eclipse usually follows the eruption of a volcano. The ash in the atmosphere absorbs the refracted sunlight that normally illuminates the surface of the moon.

Another anomaly is the appearance of bands and patches on the moon during an eclipse. The effect is created when sunlight is refracted through portions of the earth's atmosphere that are cloudy or impure. It is like light passing through a dirty lens.

Earthshine

During a lunar eclipse, when the moon is cut off from direct sunlight, its color becomes coppery. The change in color is caused by light reflected from the earth onto the surface of the moon, or what is known as "earthshine."

Both the size of the earth—it is so much bigger than the moon—and its cloudy atmosphere contribute to its ability to reflect sunlight back to the moon.

Earthshine also creates an effect called the "old moon in the new moon's arms." Early in the lunar cycle, as the crescent shape begins to appear on the right side, light from the earth is reflected onto the normally dark surface of the moon, and a golden light rings the entire moon. The scene is especially vivid on nights when the sky is clear.

fects, too, but in a much different way. The moon changes color, usually becoming coppery, sometimes deepening to red or rust.

Both types of eclipses are actually simple matters; the mystery and magic about them is in the eye of the beholder.

Eclipses occur when the moon is at a certain phase as it crosses one of two node points in its orbit around the earth. The moon's orbit is tilted about five degrees from the plane of the earth's orbit around the sun. The nodes are the two points where the moon's orbit intersects the earth's orbit.

A solar eclipse occurs when the new moon lines up directly between the sun

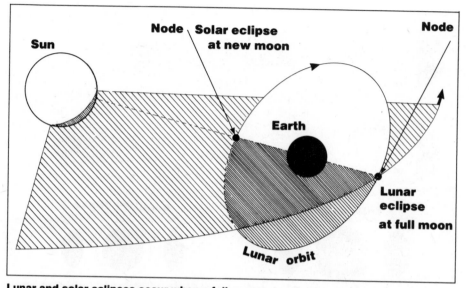

Lunar and solar eclipses occur when a full or new moon occurs at nodes, the points where lunar and earth orbits intersect.

and earth at one node, cutting off the sun's rays. The moon appears black as it passes in front of the sun. Even though the moon is much smaller than the sun, it appears to be nearly the same size in the sky because it is so much closer to the earth. The sun returns to full luminosity as the moon passes away.

A total solar eclipses is one in which the moon covers all of the sun's face. An annular total eclipse leaves visible the corona, a glorious ring of light. It occurs when the moon is farthest away

from the earth. In a partial eclipse, the moon passes over only a portion of the sun. Total solar eclipses are so spectacular that scientists and lay observers will travel thousands of miles just for a few minutes of one of nature's greatest shows.

Partial solar eclipses are much more common than total solar eclipses. All solar eclipses can be seen only from certain portions of the earth which are in the proper line of sight for the blocking effect to occur.

When lunar eclipses occur, they can

Top: Total solar eclipse occurs when moon is close to earth and completely blocks sun. Middle: Annular eclipse occurs when moon is farther away from earth and partially blocks sun. Bottom l to r: Total and annular eclipses as seen from earth.

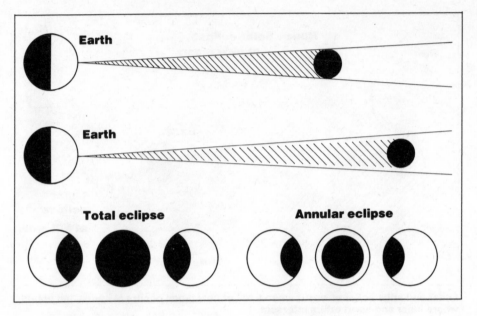

be seen from all points on the earth where the moon is visible. In a lunar eclipse, the full moon passes through the shadow of the earth at another node, cutting itself off from the sun's rays. The moon darkens in color and in some cases may seem to disappear. A lunar eclipse occurs gradually and can last for up to four hours because the earth and moon move slowly in relation to each other.

A total lunar eclipse occurs when the moon is completely engulfed by the earth's main shadow, called the umbra. The moon's color becomes copper to

Eclipse Briefs

—Solar eclipses happen no less than twice a year and no more than five times a year.

—Lunar eclipses happen no more than four times a year.

—A solar eclipse is always preceded or followed by a lunar eclipse within fourteen days.

—Eclipses occur in sequences that repeat in the "Saros cycle": every eighteen years, ten days and seven hours and forty-two minutes.

reddish and can stay that way for as long as ninety minutes. A partial eclipse is one in which the moon is only partially covered by the earth's main shadow. During a penumbral eclipse, the mildest of eclipses, the moon passes through the secondary shadow of the earth, called the penumbra. Only a portion of sun's illumination is cut off from the moon's surface.

The why and how of eclipses were unknown in earlier times; otherwise, eclipses might not have been so alarming. Throughout the world, eclipses have given birth to many myths and legends that attempt to explain the occurrences.

Native Americans believed the moon was hunted and caught by huge dogs. The Chinese believed a lunar eclipse was the work of hungry dragons that eat the moon. An ancient Scandinavian myth told of the monster Managarmer who swallowed up the moon and stained the sky with its blood.

In Rumanian folklore, eclipses are caused by creatures called *varcolaci* which eat the sun and moon. *Varcolaci* are likened to dogs, small animals like dogs, dragons, octopuslike beings with many sucking mouths, or vampires. They are also said to be spirits. Various origins are ascribed to them. They are the souls of unbaptized children or illegitimate children who have been cursed by God; they are created when someone sweeps out the house at sunset and

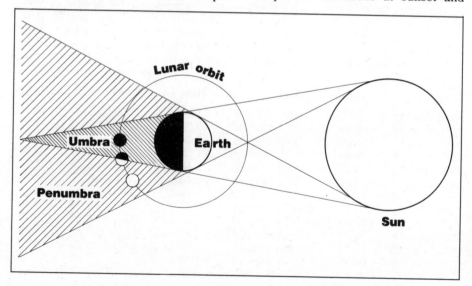

Three types of lunar eclipses: total, when moon is completely in umbra; partial, when moon is in both umbra and penumbra; and penumbral, when moon is in penumbra.

pushes the dust in the direction of the sun, or when someone makes maize porridge and accidentally puts the porridge stick into the blazing fire. Perhaps the most colorful explanation appears in I. Otescu's *Belief of the Rumanian Peasant Concerning the Sky and the Stars*:

> Others say that the *varcolaci* originate from the air of heaven, when women spin at night, especially at midnight, without a candle, especially if they cast spells with the thread they spin. Hence it is never good to spin by moonlight, for vampires and *varcolaci* get up to the sky by the thread and eat the sun and moon. They fasten themselves to the thread and the thread makes itself into a road for them. As long as the thread does not break the *varcolaci* have power, and can go wherever they wish. They attack the heavenly bodies, they bite the moon, so that she appears covered with blood, or till none of her is left. But if the thread is broken their power is broken and they go to another part of the sky.

Lunar Eclipses from 1991 to 2010

Times given are Greenwich Mean (Civil) Time. To convert to Eastern Standard Time subtract 5 hours from Greenwich Mean Time. To convert to Australian time (Sydney) add 10 hours to Greenwich Mean Time. When converting, please remember to take into account that the times will be affected by Daylight Savings Time adjustments. Daylight Savings Time varies in each time zone.

The hours given are according to the 24-hour, or "military" clock, in which the P.M. hours continue past 12 noon. For example, 2 P.M. is hour 14. To convert to the 12-hour clock, subtract 12 from the hour. For example, to figure 14:03, calculate 14 minus 12 equals 2, for 2:03 P.M.

Date	Time	Date	Time	Date	Time	Date	Time
1991 Jan 30	5:59	1996 Apr 14	0:10	2001 Jul 5	14:56	2006 Sep 7	18:51
1991 Jun 27	3:15	1996 Sep 27	2:54	2001 Dec 30	10:29	2007 Mar 3	23:21
1991 Jul 26	18:08	1997 Mar 24	4:40	2002 May 26	12:04	2007 Aug 28	10:37
1991 Dec 21	10:33	1997 Sep 16	18:46	2002 Jun 24	21:28	2008 Feb 21	3:26
1992 Jun 15	4:57	1998 Mar 13	4:22	2002 Nov 20	1:46	2008 Aug 16	21:10
1992 Dec 9	23:44	1998 Aug 8	2:25	2003 May 16	3:40	2009 Feb 9	14:38
1993 Jun 4	13:01	1998 Sep 6	11:10	2003 Nov 9	1:19	2009 Jul 7	9:39
1993 Nov 29	6:25	1999 Jan 31	16:19	2004 May 4	20:31	2009 Aug 6	0:39
1994 May 25	3:31	1999 Jul 28	11:33	2004 Oct 28	3:04	2009 Dec 31	19:23
1994 Nov 18	6:44	2000 Jan 21	4:44	2005 Apr 24	9:56	2010 Jun 26	11:39
1995 Apr 15	12:18	2000 Jul 16	13:56	2005 Oct 17	12:03	2010 Dec 21	8:17
1995 Oct 8	16:04	2001 Jan 9	20:21	2006 Mar 14	23:48		

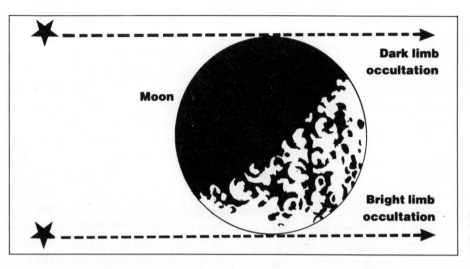

Moon

Dark limb occultation

Bright limb occultation

Grazing occultations occur when a star or planet blinks in light as it brushes a limb of the moon.

In many cultures it was common to make noise by banging gongs, pans and kettles to frighten away the dragon, demon or evil spirit that was devouring the sun or moon.

As astronomy advanced and more was understood about the nature of eclipses, it became possible to predict eclipses. Christopher Columbus, who was versed in astronomy, used his knowledge of an approaching eclipse in 1504 to win food for his men from Jamaican islanders. Columbus told the natives that if they didn't give food, he would make the moon "change her color and lose her light." When it did, the island's inhabitants were so fearful they agreed to Columbus's demands and even elevated him to the rank of a god.

Occultations

Have you ever looked up in the sky and watched as the moon seems to swallow a star? The phenomenon is known as an occultation.

Lasting for as long as an hour, or over in just a matter of minutes, occultations occur when the moon, traveling across the sky, passes in front of a star.

The effect is immediate. All of a sudden the star disappears, like a candle being snuffed out. Just as suddenly, it blinks on again when it emerges from the other side of the moon.

An occultation does not always completely block the light of a star. If the moon is less than full, the starlight remains visible. In "grazing occultations," the star appears to blink on and off as it crosses the edge of the moon, its light momentarily blocked by the peaks on the surface.

Occultations demonstrate that the moon has no atmosphere. If there were a lunar atmosphere, stars would not appear to be suddenly snuffed out when occulted by the moon. Instead, the star's light would grow dimmer as it passes through the moon's atmosphere.

Because the moon's orbital path is generally known ahead of time, occultations can be predicted. This enables observers to watch them as they occur. Dates and times of occultations are published in observers' handbooks—usually up to a tenth of a minute.

For more than two centuries professional and amateur observers have recorded seemingly impossible variations on a typical occultation. Instead of being obscured by the passing moon, occulted stars have been seen to remain fixed in the sky—almost hanging on the moon's limb for a second or two. There have been extremely rare instances when a star has appeared to pass in front of the moon for several seconds.

In 1783, an observer recorded the following incident involving the astronomer Sir William Herschel. "Mrs. Lind placed herself at a telescope and watched attentively. Scarcely had the star disappeared before Mrs. Lind thought she saw it again, and exclaimed that the star had gone in front of, not behind the moon. Finally Herschel stepped up to the telescope, and in fact he saw a bright point on the dark disc of the moon, which he followed attentively. It became fainter and finally vanished."

Other observers have recorded similar spectacles. Reports have ranged from a star "that emerged at the moon's dark limb and hung there for a few seconds" to one that hung for so long the watcher got "tired of waiting."

One observer was so mystified by an occultation that took place over the skies in Scotland in 1928 that he said it was a sight "I will never forget." After the moon and star crossed paths "the light of the star not only remained for some seconds on the edge of the moon, but it grazed about two degrees past the edge as if the star were between the moon and the earth then began to diminish and vanish."

The moon observer Patrick Moore saw a strange occultation in 1972, verified by a colleague watching at the same time. The star he was watching faded out instead of suddenly vanishing. However, as Moore wrote later, this event could be explained. "The star was a binary—a system made up of two stars, so close together to appear as one object. This explained the fading, since the two components were hidden at fractionally different times." It is likely that all instances of an apparently fading occultation are due to the presence of a binary system.

Were There Ever Lunarians?

The ancients never doubted that the moon was inhabited. All one had to do was gaze at the lunar face to see great dark areas that surely were seas. And if seas were present upon the moon, then so was air, and so was life. Plutarch, the first-century Greek essayist, declared, "The Pythagoreans affirm that the moon appears to be terrestrial, for she is inhabited, like the earth where we are, and peopled with the greatest living creatures, and the fairest plants. . . . There is nothing that proves that habitation of men in the moon is impossible."

The notion that the moon had an atmosphere was tied into the old and widespread belief that all planetary bodies had viable air. This belief was prevalent even up to the late nineteenth century. Sir David Brewster (1781–1868), writing in his book *More Worlds Than One*, intoned that "every planet and satellite in the solar system must have an atmosphere."

When the telescope was invented in the early seventeenth century, scientists turned their instruments toward the moon and saw that it was a rocky world. They still assumed that the great, dark plains were seas and that the moon was surrounded by a blanket of life-supporting air. With telescopes, they expected to see signs of life close up. Robert Hooke believed he could build a telescope powerful enough to see the moon inhabitants themselves. While no living creatures were documented, scientists nonetheless interpreted lunar features and phenomena in terms of life. The observations of apparent clouds on the moon were taken as proof of an atmosphere. John Wilkins (1614–1672) wrote, "There is an atmosphoera, or an orb of gross vaporous air, immediately encompassing the body of the moon. . . . That 'tis possible there may be inhabitants in this

other world; but of what kind we are uncertain."

Toward the end of the seventeenth century, the idea of seas was abandoned, but lunar observers still thought the moon had air and water. The existence of life on the moon was supported by many, including the illustrious English astronomer, Sir William Herschel (whose equally illustrious astronomer son, Sir John Herschel, was victimized in 1835 by a moon hoax). William Herschel stated in 1795 in *Philosophical Transactions of the Royal Society*, "While man walks upon the ground, birds fly in the air, and fishes swim in the water, we can certainly not object to the conventions afforded by the moon, if those that are to inhabit its regions are fitted to their conditions as well as

we on this globe are to ours. . . . I believe the analogies that have been mentioned fully suffice to establish the high probability of the moon's being inhabited like the earth."

Others of the seventeenth and eighteenth centuries were more certain that not only was there life on the moon, but that it was lush and luxuriant. "The moon is inhabited by rational creatures, and . . . its surface is more or less covered with a vegetation not very dissimilar to our own earth," declared H. W. M. Olbers, a German scientist. The German astronomer Franz von Gruithuisen claimed to observe through his telescope "great artificial works on the moon erected by the lunarians" and "a system of fortifications thrown up by the selenitic engineers." Another Ger-

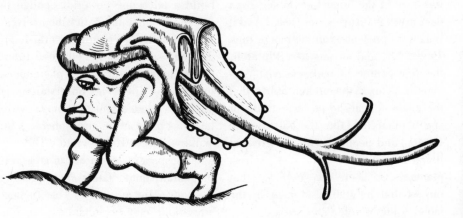

Moon Falls over Missouri!

One night in October 1939, between 7:30 and 8 o'clock, residents around Springfield, Missouri were astonished to see the full moon suddenly lose its place and fall through the sky, flaming like a meteor. On October 22, headlines in the *Springfield News and Leader* trumpeted, "Extra! The Moon Falls on Strafford Route Three!"

One witness testified that the moon "looked to be about one or two hours high when it just suddenly turned over and fell like a star would fall, making a ball of fire which could be seen down low for five or ten minutes. No one around here ever heard of the moon falling, even people fifty years old. Some wouldn't believe it."

And right those doubters were. It turned out that the flaming ball wasn't the moon, after all. It was a weather balloon meeting its demise as it fell through the atmosphere.

Furthermore, The moon wasn't even full that night. At the time of the incident, the moon was a barely visible waxing sickle just over the horizon.

---

man astronomer, M. Schroeter, said that the atmosphere he saw on the moon proved that the moon must bear intelligent beings. They further enjoyed uniform temperatures, he said, no storms, and light vapors rising from the lunar valleys and falling as dew to fertilize the fields.

Not only scientists believed in life on the moon. Emanuel Swedenborg, the eighteenth-century Swedish mystic, knew the moon was inhabited through his alleged conversations with angels and his trips out-of-body to visit other realities. The moon beings were not creatures, but humans, he declared. "That there are inhabitants in the moon is well known to spirits and angels, and in like manner that there are inhabitants in the moons or satellites which revolve around Jupiter and Saturn," Swedenborg said. "They who have not seen and discoursed with spirits from those moons shall entertain no doubt but that there are men inhabiting them, because they are earths alike with the planets, and wherever an earth is, there are men inhabitants; for man is the end for which every earth was created, and nothing was made by the great Creator without an end."

All of these declarations were backed up by no evidence, save for the observation of what appeared to be clouds on the lunar surface. The bubble grew to monstrous proportions in 1835, when a life-on-the-moon hoax was perpetrated by a journalist.

In the late nineteenth and early twentieth centuries, it became evident that the moon supported no earthlike creatures. Research showed that the moon did have an atmosphere, but that it was extremely tenuous. More powerful telescopes and unmanned lunar probes revealed no signs of life.

But does the moon support organisms too small to be detected by distant observations? If not now, did it ever? The questions were not completely laid to rest until the manned Apollo moon missions of the 1960s and 1970s. Lunar rocks and soil brought back for analysis showed no evidence of organic material. The moon is and always has been a dead world.

The question of the moon's atmosphere was answered by the Apollo 17 mission of December 1972. Astronauts Eugene Cernan and Harrison (Jack) Schmitt set up a mass spectrometers and found that the moon's atmosphere is comprised of "collisionless gas," in which the atomic components move around freely. The lunar air is comprised of hydrogen, helium, neon and argon, the last of which freezes at night and is released at dawn. The atmosphere, which is so thin that for all practical purposes the moon may be called airless, is thought to derive from solar wind, a stream of ionized particles sent out from the sun.

Moon Gazers

Galileo Galilei (1564–1642). Italian astronomer and mathematician, Galileo was the first to use a telescope. He was persecuted by the Catholic Church for his defense of Copernicus's theory that the sun, not the earth, was the center of the solar system. He mapped the moon and attempted to measure its mountains.

William Lower (circa 1611). Although little is known about his life, Lower is believed to be the first British astronomer. A contemporary of Galileo, he is said to have used one of the Italian's telescopes, called a "perspective cylinder," to study the moon.

Giambattista Riccioli (1598–1671). Jesuit professor of astronomy and theology at the University of Bologna. Riccioli named the plains *maria* after seas, and named other features after prominent scientists and philosophers.

Johan Hewlecke, also **Hevelius** (1611–1687). Wealthy seventeenth-century astronomer who built an observatory on the roof of his house and furnished it with some of the best equipment available. Noted for the first detailed map of the moon and for discovering that the lunar seas are really great plains.

Jean Dominique Cassini (1625–1712). Director of the Paris Observatory, rebuilt in 1669. Cassini mapped the moon and also improved the early theory of librations.

Sir William Herschel (1738–1822). The "father of modern astronomy," Herschel was the first president of the Royal Astronomical Society. He discovered Uranus and also was convinced the moon was habitable.

Johann Hieronymous Schroeter (1754–1816). The founder of the modern science of moon study, or selenography. He devoted much of his life to making moon drawings that were considered quite valuable.

Johann Heinrich Mädler (1794–1874). Mädler, along with Wilhelm Beer (1797–1850), authored *Mappa Selenographica* and *Der Mond,* two outstanding works that detailed the surface of the moon.

Lewis Rutherfurd (1816–1892). An American lawyer who became one of the pioneers of lunar photography.

Julius Schmidt (1825–1884). German astronomer known for his lunar map, 72 inches (182.88 cm) in diameter, that nearly matched the quality of the first modern charts.

Henry Draper (1837–1882). Draper was a lunar photographer whose pictures were of considerable use in the study of the moon.

Edmund Neison (1851–1938). At the age of twenty-five, Neison published *The Moon*, which contained a two-foot map that updated the earlier work of Mädler and Beer. Neison's map described every moon formation then known.

William Henry Pickering (1858–1938). A distinguished American lunar and planetary astronomer, Pickering made a number of important observations of the moon and helped set up several major observatories.

Bernard Lyot (1897–1952). Considered one of the world's greatest astronomers, Lyot did major research concerning the moon's surface and produced top quality lunar photographs with his colleague, Audouin Dollfus.

Read All about It! Life on the Moon!

In August 1835, the *New York Sun* announced the astonishing news that life on the moon had been discovered by the respected English astronomer, Sir John Herschel, who had taken a large telescope with him to the Cape of Good Hope in 1833. Herschel had re-

ported his momentous findings in the *Edinburgh Journal of Science*, the *Sun* alleged.

In a series of articles, reporter Richard A. Locke told how Herschel, using a powerful telescope that could magnify objects 42,000 times, had observed 16 species of animals, 38 species of trees and 76 species of plants, including great fields of poppies. The animals included horned bears, two-footed beavers with no tails, elk, reindeerlike creatures and buffalo, the latter of which had fleshy hoods over their eyes to protect them from the extremes of light and dark. Locke also described 60-foot high amethysts and a sapphire temple.

Most incredible of all, Locke said that Herschel had seen a humanoid race of bat-beings four feet in stature with yellow skin, copper hair and wings. Their faces were "a slight improvement upon that of the large orangoutang." The bat-beings flew about and appeared intelligent, judging from their facial expressions and the way they conversed.

The articles caused the *Sun*'s circulation to skyrocket, just as Locke had intended. He had fabricated the stories, using a few partial truths, to save the declining paper from demise. It was

Copies of the *New York Sun* were snapped up by readers eager to learn about the strange lunarians.

true that Herschel was using a new, powerful telescope, but it was much smaller and thousands of times less powerful than what Locke claimed. It was also true that there had existed an *Edinburgh Journal of Science*, but it had ceased publication in 1833. Everything else was pure fantasy.

In a day when communication was much slower that it is now, Locke could get away with his stories unchallenged for a time. Many in the public on both sides of the Atlantic believed the articles—even the venerable *New York Times* was taken in. The *Sun* sold by the thousands for several days, and when the articles were printed as a pamphlet, 60,000 were snapped up at once. An enthusiastic American preacher told his congregation that he expected to be selling Bibles soon to the inhabitants of the moon. Perhaps it was Dr. Dwight, a theologian who proclaimed, "it is most rationally concluded that intelligent beings in great multitudes inhabit her regions, being far better and happier than ourselves."

Inevitably, the hoax was exposed. A

rival paper carried the story within a few days. Locke was caught off guard in his office by a delegation of Yale University scientists who demanded to see Herschel's reports. There were none, of course, but Locke stalled the scientists by claiming he had sent them to the printer. The ensuing crazy chase had Locke and scientists racing all over New York. Locke took a shortcut and hurried ahead of the scientists to the printer's, where he convinced a man to tell the scientists the reports had been sent to another printer. Meanwhile, Locke ran on to that printer. Locke at last was forced to admit he had no original papers. The *Sun* confessed publicly to the hoax on September 16, and Locke was forced to resign from the *Sun* in disgrace.

Fantasies die hard, however, and months passed before the stories were finally squelched. Herschel, gazing away on the other side of the world, did not hear of the matter for two to three months. When he did, he was gracious about the hoax, but vigorously denied the claims.

Once in a Blue Moon

Blue moons are not just the stuff of imagination and fantasy—they are real. They occur when dust particles and pollution in the earth's atmosphere filter more light at the red end of the color spectrum than at the blue end. The longer wavelengths, including red and yellow, scatter, while the shorter wavelengths, including blue and green, intensify. This gives the moon a blue or green appearance against the night sky, especially if it is low on the horizon, where its light is subject to the greatest refraction by the atmosphere. Dust from Canadian forest fires caused a famous blue moon on September 26, 1950. Similarly, the moon "turned" blue following the huge volcanic eruption of Krakatoa in 1883.

Full moons that occur twice in the same calendar month are also called blue moons. Because the lunar cycle is 29.5 days, the phases of the moon gradually slip backward through the progression of the Gregorian calendar until a full moon appears on or near the beginning of the month and again before the end of the month. These blue moons occur roughly every 2.5 years, and are most likely to occur in the months with 31 days: January, March, May, July, August, October and December. Blue moons never occur in February and are rare in the 30-day months of April, June, September and November.

On August 27, 1883, Krakatoa erupted and spewed such an enormous quantity of debris and smoke into the air that the moon turned blue. The eruption was heard 3,000 miles (4,824 kilometers) away, and killed 36,000 people.

Moon Facts

Diameter: 2,160 miles/3,476 kilometers (0.27 of earth's diameter)

Circumference: 6,790 miles/10,930 kilometers

Mean radius: 1,080 miles/1,738 kilometers

Mean distance from earth: 238,857 miles/382,176 kilometers

Maximum distance from earth (apogee): 252,710 miles/404,336 kilometers

Minimum distance from earth (perigee): 221,463 miles/354,340 kilometers

Surface temperature range: 273° F (130° C) day; −244° F (−153° C) night

Mass: 8 X 10^{19} tons/7.35 x 10^{22} kilograms; 0.0123 earth's mass; 3.7 x 10^{-8} sun's mass

Volume: 0.0204 earth's volume

Density: 3.34 times more dense than water

Atmospheric density (maximum possible): 1 x 10^{-4} earth

Surface area: 15 million square miles/24.13 million square kilometers

Surface gravity: 5.31 feet² per second; 0.165 times that of earth

Escape velocity: 1.48 miles per second/2.38 kilometers per second

Mean orbital speed: 2,287 miles per hour/3,680 kilometers per hour

Sidereal period: 27 days, 7 hours, 43 minutes, 11.5 seconds

Synodic period: 29 days, 12 hours, 44 minutes, 2.9 seconds

Orbital direction: Counterclockwise

Mean motion of terminator in longitude per day: 11.49°, or 216.4716 miles at earth's equator

Mean inclination to lunar equator: 6° 4′

Mean orbital inclination to ecliptic: 5° 08′ 43″

Inclination of moon's equator to ecliptic orbit: 10° 35′

Mean eccentricity of orbit: 0.0549 (earth is 0.0167)

Revolution of nodes: 18 years, 10 days, 8 hours, 30 minutes; or 18.5995 years

Saros cycle: 18 years, 10 days, 7 hours, 42 minutes

Area of surface always seen: 0.589 of whole surface, of which 0.178 is due to librations

Area of surface never seen: 0.411 of whole surface

Radius of polar regions: 24 miles (38.6 kilometers)

Parallax: 0.9507°

Average albedo (percent of sunlight reflected): 7 (earth's albedo: 40)

Lunar Glossary

Albedo. The power of a celestial body to reflect light, calculated by dividing the amount of light reflected by the amount of light falling on the body.

Anomalistic month. 27.55455 days, the amount of time it takes the moon to return to the point in its orbit when it is either closest or farthest from the earth.

Aphelion. The point in a planet's orbit that is farthest away from the sun.

Apogee. The point in the moon's orbit that is farthest from the earth.

Apolune. The point at which a spacecraft circling the moon is farthest from the lunar surface.

Celestial equator. An imaginary circle that extends from the earth's equator into space.

Celestial sphere. An imaginary sphere that has the stars as its inner surface and earth at its center, used for mapping positions of celestial bodies.

Conjunction. The position of two celestial bodies that have the same longitude in the celestial sphere. Also refers to the point at which the moon is between the sun and earth.

Ecliptic. The path that the sun appears to take in the celestial sphere. Or, an imaginary circle on the terrestrial globe that is at an angle of approximately 23 degrees and 7 minutes to the equator.

Lacus. A portion of the moon's surface, said to look like a small lake.

Latitude. A measurement, on a sphere, that uses imaginary lines that run parallel to the equator. The equator is located at 0 degrees and the poles are at 90 degrees north and south.

Limb. The outer edge of the "disk" of the moon.

Longitude. A measurement, on a sphere, that uses imaginary lines that run at right angles to the equator, converging at the poles.

Mare. On the moon, a dark area formed from lava flows. From the Latin word for "sea."

Mons. Mountain.

Montes. Mountain range.

Nadir. Relative to an observer on earth, the point exactly opposite the zenith.

Node. The point at which the orbit of a moon or planet intersects the ecliptic.

Opposition. An alignment in which the earth is between the sun and the moon, causing the moon to be 180 degrees from the sun, relative to earth.

Palus. A dark section of the moon that has a swamplike appearance.

Parallax. An apparent change in the position of an object viewed from the earth resulting from a change in the position of the observer.

Perigee. The point in the moon's orbit closest to the earth.

Perihelion. The point of a planet's orbit that is closest to the sun.

Perilune. The point at which an orbiting object (satellite or spaceship) is closest to the moon's surface.

Regression of nodes. The shift of nodes in a westward direction.

Rille. A canyon or small valley. Also known as a rima.

Rupes. Fault.

Saros cycle. A cycle of 18 years, 10 days, 7 hours and 42 minutes, during which the moon moves to the same position relative to the sun, its perigee and the nodes. Eclipses are predicted using the Saros cycle.

Selenography. The scientific study of the moon's surface.

Selenology. The science of moon study.

Sidereal month. 27.32166 days, the time it takes the moon to complete its rotation around the earth and return to its starting position, using a fixed star as a reference point.

Sinus. An area of the moon's surface that looks like an ocean bay.

Synodic month. 29.5309 days, the period between one new moon to the next.

Terminator. The line of division between the light and dark portions of the moon.

Vallis. Valley.

Zenith. Relative to an observer on earth, the point in the sky that is directly overhead.

Moon Myths and Other Tales

Science has its facts and theories, but we get another perspective on the moon—and in many ways a more satisfying one—from the world of mythology and legend. Mythology tells the story of the creation of the cosmos and world, how all living things came to be, and why everything is the way it is. Myth explains the order of the universe, including why the sun rises and sets and why the moon rises and sets. Legends are popularized myths and stories that become embellished and embroidered as they are told and retold through generations. The moon plays a role in many legends about the escapades and exploits of various figures. The moon also figures in folk tales and nursery rhymes, which are broken-down versions of myths, told for entertainment or to instill community values.

Moon tales lift us up into a magical realm where imagination rules and the hard facts of science become alien. The moon and animals speak, people fly and climb into the sky, the moon comes down and captures people—anything in our wildest dreams can happen. Moon tales never lose their magic, no matter how often they are told, no matter how old the listener.

A selection of moon myths and other tales and rhymes are presented here to explain how the moon came to be in the sky, how the dark marks were made on its surface and why eclipses happen. There are also some "just-so" stories in which the moon creates other phenomena or in which people have great adventures involving the moon. Some of the myths and legends are taken from the lore of Native Americans.

Creation Stories

All mythologies address cosmogony, the explanation of how the universe and all things in it came to be. Central to all cosmogonies are the creation of the world and its two most important celestial bodies, the sun and the moon; the creation of all living things; how human beings emerged in to the world; and how they acquired the knowledge necessary to survive in the world.

Creation stories probably came into being in response to observations of the quality and behavior of beings and objects around them. People noticed that the moon had no light of its own, changed its shape on a predictable basis, and seemed to move unsteadily in the sky. Lunar creation stories appear in diverse mythologies.

Odin's Chariots: A Norse Myth

In the beginning was Audhumla, whose name means "rich, hornless cow." She was the primeval cow, formed from vapors. She lived by licking salt from stones, and she fed the primeval giant, Ymir. One day as she licked the stones, a man's hair appeared, and by the third day, a whole man was formed. This was Buri.

Buri married Bestla, a daughter of Bolthor, one of the frost giants. They had three sons, Odin, Vili and Ve. Odin became chief of the Aesir gods.

> ### Born of a Calabash: A Hawaiian Creation Myth
>
> The first gods were Ku, Ka-ne, Lono and Kanaloa, who came from a far-off land. They brought with them a mysterious people who live in the precipices and trees and rocks. These people became the invisible spirits of the air. The earth was a calabash, a large, round gourd. The gods threw the calabash up, and it became the sky. Part of the thick flesh of the calabash became the sun, and part of it became the moon. The seeds formed the stars.

Odin and his brothers hated Ymir and the other frost giants. They attacked and killed Ymir. His copious blood flooded out and drowned all the other frost giants save two.

Odin, Vili and Ve then shaped the world from the body of Ymir. They made mountains from bones and seas and lakes from blood. They made the sky from Ymir's skull. They took glowing embers and sparks and made them into sun, moon and stars, and gave each its proper place in the sky. Some were fixed and some were free to move about.

From two fallen trees with their roots ripped out, an ash and an elm, the sons made first man and first woman, and gave them gifts of life, knowledge and feelings. Odin then took a daughter and a son of the giants, Night and Day, respectively, and set them in the sky on horses.

A man named Mundilfari had two children so beautiful that he called his son Moon and his daughter Sun. Odin, his brothers and their offspring, the Aesir, were so outraged at this daring that they snatched the children and placed them in the sky to guide the chariots of the sun and moon. Moon leads the way and decides when the moon will wax and wane. He is accompanied by two children in the moon, Bil and Hjuki, whom he kidnapped (see "The Children in the Moon"). Moon is forever chased by the wolf Hati. Sun follows Moon and is always in a hurry because she is chased by another wolf, Skoll. The wolves are the sons of a giantess, and they seek endlessly to eat sun and moon. They will succeed in the end, at the Ragnarok, or Twilight of the Gods.

Ka-Ne Restores the Moon: A Maori Myth

Somewhere beyond the horizon, or in the cloud-land above the heavens, there exists a land known as "the land of the water of life of the gods." In this land is a lake called the living water of Ka-ne, which has the power to restore life. When the moon dies she goes to the living water of Ka-ne, to the water which can restore all life, and can even restore the moon to its path in the sky.

In the meantime, the wolves occasionally manage to take a bite out of the sun or moon (causing eclipses). The people below shout and beat kettles and pans together in order to frighten the sky wolves away.

P'an Ku Creates the Universe: A Chinese Taoist Myth

P'an Ku created the universe out of the primordial chaos. He was the offspring of yin and yang, the dual powers of nature, and was dwarflike in stature with horns on his head. He was assisted in his great labors by the unicorn, the phoenix, the tortoise and the dragon.

P'an Ku spent 18,000 years creating the sun and the moon, the stars, the heavens and the earth. He put all things in the lower world in order, but neglected to set sun and moon on proper courses through the sky. So, the sun and moon went down into the Han Sea and left the world in darkness.

The Terrestrial Emperor sent an officer, Terrestrial Time, to order the sun and moon to move through the heavens and create day and night. They refused.

The situation required the divine intervention of Buddha. At Buddha's direction, P'an Ku wrote the character for "sun" on his left hand and the character

Yin and yang, the primal forces of the cosmos in Chinese cosmology and philosophy, are symbolized by the black and white disk, upper left. Yin, the black, represents the feminine/ passive principle. Yang, the white, represents the masculine/ active principle. They are in constant ebb and flow. Each contains a dot of the other, a representation that all life has within it both primal forces.

In a Chinese legend the T'ang
Emperor Ming visits the moon
for pleasure.

for "moon" on his right. He went to the Han Sea. He raised his left hand and called the sun, then raised his right hand and called the moon. He repeated a charm seven times. The sun and moon rose into the sky, and divided day and night.

Why the Moon Weaves a Strange Path through the Sky: A Navajo Myth

The Navajo of the southwestern United States have an enchanting explanation for how the moon was placed

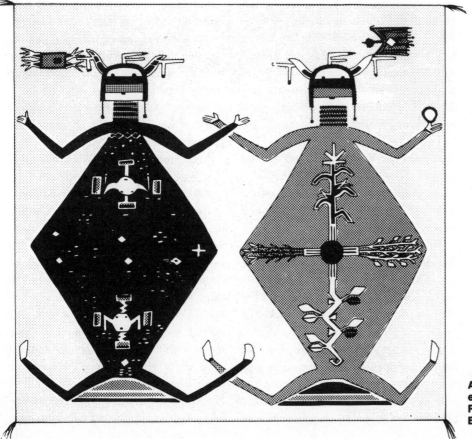

A Navajo rug design from the early twentieth century shows Father Sky, left, and Mother Earth.

in the sky, and why, compared to the sun, it weaves an irregular path across the heavens. According to one version of the Navajo emergence myth, the First People came out from the underworld to the surface of the earth. To dispel the darkness, First Man and First Woman made the sun and the moon from a slab of quartz crystal, which they fashioned into disks. They decorated the sun disk with a mask of blue turquoise that would give off heat and light. They attached red coral around the disk's rims and to its earlobes. They also attached eagle, lark and flicker feathers to spread the light and heat in the four directions. First Man and First Woman attached the sun disk to the eastern sky with lightning darts. Then they decorated the moon disk with crystal and white shell and attached it to the sky.

The disks were stationary, however, and people soon complained that there was too much heat in the east and not enough in the west. First Man and First Woman had no idea of how to make the disks move through the sky.

They were rescued by two wise old men who appeared and offered to give their spirits to the disks in order to animate them. There still was another problem: what paths to follow across the sky? First Man observed that the eagle is guided by his tail feathers, and so he attached twelve eagle feathers to each disk to point them to the correct paths in the sky (the twelve feathers are associated with the zodiac).

Sun began his journey across the sky. As he was setting, Moon began his journey. Just then, Wind Boy tried to help Moon along by blowing on him. Instead, he blew Moon's eagle feathers across his face, so that Moon could not see where he was going. As a result, Moon has an irregular path across the sky.

Another Navajo myth tells a different story of how the sun and moon were placed in the sky.

First Man and First Woman decided that lights in the sky would make the world brighter. All the People gathered sacred things to make the sun and the moon: white and yellow pollen, rainbows, rays and turquoise. The sun was fashioned from a clear stone and rimmed with turquoise and rays of red rain, sheet lightning and snakes. The People covered it with pollen and sang sacred songs. They then made the moon from crystal, which they rimmed with white shells. They covered the face with sheet lightning and water. The People covered the moon with pollen and sang the appropriate sacred songs.

Native American bowl figures from the Southwestern United States depict the opposites of light and dark.

Next the People held a council to decide what to do with the lights they had created. They thought of putting them on top of Tsoodzil (a sacred mountain) and turning them over to the Spirit People for operation, but this was rejected because the mountaintop could not be seen by all the world.

The East Wind finally convinced the People to bring the sun and moon to his

49

land. First Man appointed a young man to carry the sun across the sky every day upon his back. The young man agreed but said he did not want to be separated from his father. First Man then appointed the old man to carry the moon, which is why the moon moves more slowly and erratically than the sun.

Both son and father were given rainbows to help them in their task. The People were in sorrow to see them depart, but First Man told them not to mourn, for they would be seen in the heavens.

After arriving in the sky, Sun Bearer busied himself with making his house and did not move, but stayed directly overhead. The Moon Carrier grew weaker and weaker. On the third day, First Man directed Sun Bearer to move, and also to create some earth animals. Sun Bearer complied.

But on the fifth day after the People entered the Fifth World, the sun stopped overhead and broiled everything below. Coyote, who had invented death by tossing a stone in the water, announced that Sun Bearer wished to be paid for his task. "He demands a human life for every day that he labors and he will not move again until someone dies," Coyote said. Soon a woman died, and the sun began to move.

That night, the moon stopped at the zenith and made the same demand, relayed to the People by Coyote. Almost immediately a man died, and the moon continued on.

So it is that someone must die every day and every night in order for the sun and moon to make their journeys across the sky. And that is why the People were told not to mourn the son and his father, for everyone who died would join them in the heavens and become theirs in exchange for their precious light.

The Man in the Moon

Since human beings first looked up in the night sky and pondered the mysteries of the moon, they have seen images engraved on the lunar face. One of the most common images perceived is that of the "man in the moon."

This lunar man has been described as a peasant bearing a bundle of twigs on his back, sometimes accompanied by a dog. Shakespeare, in *A Midsummer Night's Dream*, said, "This man with lantern, dog and bush of thorns, presenteth moonshine."

How did the man in the moon get there? One explanation, given in the play *Timon*, written about 1600, offered this conundrum: "The man in the moone is not in the moone superficially, although he bee in the moone (as the Greekes will have it) catapodially, specificatively, and quidditatively." Precisely.

Many explanations for how the man got to the moon cite sin or crime. The origin of some of these tales is found in the Bible, Numbers 15:32–36. The verses tell of a man who gathered sticks on the sabbath and was stoned to death by an angry mob. The Bible makes no mention of the moon, but later embellishments in European folktales say the man was banished to the moon instead of killed. An old German version runs:

Ages ago there went one Sunday an old man into the woods to hew sticks. He cut a faggot and slung it on a stout staff, cast it over his shoulder, and began to trudge home with his burthen. On his way he met a handsome man in Sunday suit, walking towards the church. The man stopped and asked the faggot-bearer, "Do you know that this is Sunday on earth, when all must rest from their labors?" "Sunday on earth, or Monday in heaven, it's all one to me!" laughed the woodcutter. "Then bear your bundle for ever!" answered the stranger. "And as you value your Sunday on earth, yours shall be perpetual moonday in heaven; you shall stand for eternity in the moon, a warning to all Sabbath-breakers." Thereupon the stranger vanished, and the man was caught up with his staff and faggot into the moon, where he stands yet.

In another version of the story, the man is given the choice of burning in the sun or freezing in the moon. He chooses the moon. In yet another version, the culprit is a man who on Christmas Eve steals cabbages from his neighbor's garden. The villagers catch him and conjure him up to the moon, where he can still be seen with his cabbages. A variation of that story says that the man used cabbages to steal sheep.

Numerous other explanations are given for the man in the moon. He is Judas, exiled for his betrayal of Christ, or Isaac carrying wood for the sacrifice of himself on Mount Moriah, or Cain carrying thorns, to offer God the cheapest gift from the field. In Hebrew lore, the man in the moon is Jacob. Panamanian lore says the man was sent there as punishment for incest. The Caddo Na-tive Americans, in the southeastern United States, tell of a brother who committed incest with his sister in the dark. She smeared paint on his face so that he could be identified later. He became the man in the moon.

According to a German tale, the man in the moon is really a man and a woman. The man was guilty of strewing brambles and thorns across the path of church-goers, and the woman was guilty of churning butter on Sunday. He appears in the moon carrying his thorns, while she holds her butter tub. Another legend from northern Europe says the man in the moon carries a tar bucket, with which he tarred marks on the moon. Some Native American tribes see a man and his dog.

In Malaysia, the man in the moon is a hunchback sitting under a banyan tree making a fishing line. The line is being eaten at the other end by a rat. Malaysian lore says this is good, for if the hunchback is allowed to finish his line, he will use it to fish everything on the earth up to the moon.

In New Guinea, the image is not that of a man, but the finger marks of mischievous boys. The moon was kept in a jar by an old woman. The boys opened the jar and tried unsuccessfully to grab the moon as it escaped.

The people of Rantum, a tiny island community off the northwestern coast of Germany, associated the man in the moon with the tides. The man was a giant who caused the tide to come in by stooping to scoop up lunar waters which he poured onto the earth. At ebb tide, he stood erect and rested from his work, allowing the water to flow back.

Whatever the reason for the man being in the moon, it is considered impolite, unlucky and even a grievous sin to point at him, for he will not stand for the insult. Do so and you will not go to heaven, according to Yorkshire superstition, while in Derbyshire you can get away with it six times, but on the seventh you will be struck blind.

When he is not insulted, the man in the moon is a jolly, claret-drinking fellow, according to old English ballads, two versions of which follow.

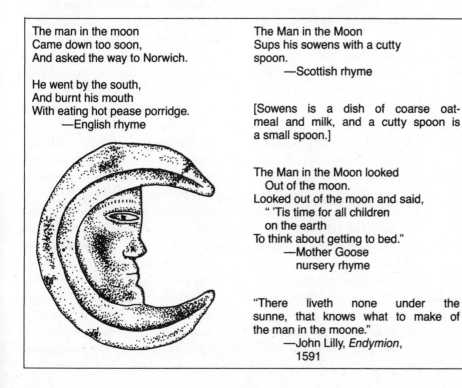

The man in the moon
Came down too soon,
And asked the way to Norwich.

He went by the south,
And burnt his mouth
With eating hot pease porridge.
—English rhyme

The Man in the Moon
Sups his sowens with a cutty
spoon.
—Scottish rhyme

[Sowens is a dish of coarse oatmeal and milk, and a cutty spoon is a small spoon.]

The Man in the Moon looked
    Out of the moon.
Looked out of the moon and said,
    " 'Tis time for all children
    on the earth
To think about getting to bed."
—Mother Goose
    nursery rhyme

"There liveth none under the sunne, that knows what to make of the man in the moone."
—John Lilly, *Endymion*,
1591

The man in the moon drinks claret,
  But he is a dull Jack-a-Dandy;
Would he know a sheep's head from a
  carrot
  He should learn to drink cyder and
  brandy.

Our man in the moon drinks clarret,
  With powder-beef, turnep, and
  carret.
  If he doth so, why should not you
  Drink until the sky looks blew?

The Woman in the Moon

Traditions that the spots seen from the earth on the moon portray not a man but a woman or a girl exist in tribal lore around the world.

Samoans look at the moon and see Sina and her child, mallet and board. According to legend, Sina was out one evening at twilight with her child, beating out bark to make cloth. It was during a famine, and the rising moon looked like delicious breadfruit. Sina said, "Why can you not come down and let my child have a bit of you?" The indignant moon swept down and took up Sina, her child and work tools. They remain on the moon's face.

A similar belief is held among the Tonga, who see a woman in the moon sitting down and beating bark. The Kwakiutl of the Pacific Northwest see a girl with a bucket. The Shawnee of southeastern United States see a woman bending over a cooking pot, with her little dog nearby. In the Cook Islands, the image is said to be that of a girl making tapa, a paperlike cloth made by pounding the inner bark of the paper mulberry tree. The stones holding down the tapa are visible; when the girl pushes aside the stones, it thunders.

In Mangaia, an island in the Hervey group, the woman is Ina, making a cloth of white clouds to be sailed into the sky. According to myth, Ina took a mortal husband, but after many happy years sent him back to earth on a rainbow, so that the moon would not be defiled by death.

The Maori see a grumbling old woman who complained when the moon went behind a cloud just as she went to fetch water. The moon seized her, her water gourd and her basket, as well as the tree to which she clung in vain. The woman and all these things are visible in the markings, or dark areas, on the moon's face. Another version of the New Zealand myth replaces the old woman with Rona, a girl who insulted the moon when a cloud obscured the moon's light, causing her to stumble. The offended moon raced down out of

the sky, grabbed her and tore her away from a bush.

Another complaining woman myth is told by the Iroquois, a Woodlands tribe of northeastern United States. The Iroquois say that the marks are a woman banished to the moon because of her constant complaining that she could not prophesy the end of the world. There, she weaves while her cat sits beside her. Once a month she puts the weaving aside to stir a kettle of boiling maize porridge. Her cat takes the opportunity to undo all of her weaving. The woman is doomed to start over every month until the end of time, when she will finally finish her task.

The Chams of Cambodia identify the woman in the moon as Pajan Yan, the goddess of healing, who was banished to the moon before she could heal and restore to life all the dead.

The Creek, of southeastern United States, say that the marks show a child brought to the moon by Woman in the Moon. One night the child awoke and asked her mother for water. The mother was too sleepy to respond. Feeling sorry for the child, Woman in the Moon came down to earth and said, "Here is water from the sky to drink." The child drank the water, and agreed to go home with Woman in the Moon. The spots show

the child and also a little basket she held in her hand the night she went to the moon.

Some woman-in-the-moon legends are variations on the incest theme, in which the moon is a sister who is victimized by her incestuous brother, the sun. According to a legend of the Inuit, who live in parts of Alaska, Siberia, Canada, and Greenland, the marks are ashes. The sun stole into his sister's bed at night, and she put ashes on her hand to mark him. Ever after, the sun chases the moon through the sky.

The Masai of Africa see the sun and moon as husband and wife who quarrel. After their fights, the sun shines brightly in shame, while the moon shows marks of a missing eye and a swollen lip.

Classical and European folk beliefs about the woman in the moon do exist, but are less prevalent than those about the man in the moon. One folktale holds that the woman is Mary Magdalene, while another likens the moon's changing phases to feminine cycles and

> On Saturday night I lost my wife,
> And where do you think I found her?
> Up in the moon, singing a tune,
> And all the stars around her.
> —Mother Goose nursery rhyme

whims. Plutarch told the story of the moon asking her mother to make her a petticoat to fit the proportions of her body. The mother replied, "Why, how is it possible that I should knit or weave one to fit well about thee considering that I see thee one while full, another while croissant or in the wane and pointed with tips of horns, and sometimes again half round?"

The Daughter of the Moon and the Son of the Sun: A Russian Myth

One day Peivalké-Sunbeam, the son of the sun, went to his father and told him the time had come for him to marry. Alas, he was at a loss for a bride, for he had tried his golden boots on all the maids who lived upon the earth, but none could wear them, nor fly through the air.

The sun said he would ask the moon, who had just given birth to a daughter. They were poorer than the sun and Peivalké, but at least they lived in the sky.

The sun waited for a day when the moon rose in the morning, and put his proposition to her. The moon was alarmed. Her infant was so small—how could she marry? The sun waived the moon's objections aside. Her daughter, he said, would grow up in his own wealthy house, where she would be well fed. "Come, let my son Peivalké see her," said the sun.

"Oh, no!" said the moon, protesting that Peivalké would scorch her delicate daughter. Then she announced that the child was already betrothed to Nainas of the northern lights.

The sun became angry and threw a temper tantrum, creating thunder, howling winds and high waves that crashed in from the sea. The earth trembled and people huddled inside their *vezhas*, their summer homes.

The moon decided to hide her daughter. She chose an old man and his wife who lived on an island in a lake. The couple found a silver cradle hanging from a fir branch. It was empty, yet a child's voice said, "Niekia—I'm not here! And now—here I am!" And the child appeared in the cradle.

The overjoyed couple took the baby home and raised her lovingly into a fine, shining young maid. They called her Niekia because whenever she wanted to play, she would say, "Niekia—I'm not here!" and vanish. At night she would go outside and reach up toward the moon, and shine brightly.

Eventually the sun heard about a

maid of unmatched beauty who lived on the island. He sent his son to investigate. Peivalké immediately fell in love with Niekia. But when she tried on his golden boots, she was scorched. Nonetheless, Peivalké intended to carry her away, but she vanished.

Niekia hid in the forest, and when the moon rose, she followed the beams to an empty house on the shore of the lake. It was dirty inside, and Niekia set about cleaning everything. When she finished, she turned into an old spindle and fell asleep.

At dusk she was awakened by silver warriors who entered the house. They were the northern lights brothers, including her true betrothed, Nainas. They were impressed by the cleanliness, and Nainas called out asking for their unknown helper to show herself. If she was younger than he, Nainas would make her his bride. Niekia revealed herself and shyly agreed to marry Nainas. Just then the sun rose, and the northern lights had to leave.

Every evening the northern lights came to their home, where they played war games that caused great flashing lights of color in the sky, and every dawn they flew away.

Niekia pondered how to keep Nainas with her during the day. She made a dark curtain of reindeer skin embroidered with the Milky Way, and hung it over the ceiling of the house to disguise the coming of the dawn.

That night, Nainas overslept. When it was daylight, Niekia went outside, but inadvertently let sunlight stream through the door. When Nainas ran out in a panic, the sun saw him and pinned him to the ground. Niekia rushed to Nainas and covered him with her body, enabling him to escape. He melted into the sky.

The sun grabbed Niekia and burned her with his fierce gaze. He summoned Peivalké. Weeping, Niekia refused to marry Peivalké, even though the sun might kill her. The enraged sun flung her back into the arms of the moon.

Her mother caught her and pressed her to her heart, where she remains today. The shadow of her face is still visible upon the moon. At night Niekia watches, with great longing, the northern lights in their spectacular battles in the sky.

How the Moon Got Spots and Ate the Sun: A Zambesi Myth

Formerly the moon was very pale and did not shine, and was jealous of the sun with its glittering feathers of light.

She took advantage of a moment when the sun was looking at the other side of the earth, and stole some of his feathers of fire to adorn herself. But the sun found out, and in his anger splashed the moon with mud which remains stuck to it for all eternity.

Since then the moon has been bent on vengeance. Every ten years she surprises the sun when he is off guard, and cunningly splatters him with mud. Then the sun shows large spots and for some hours cannot shine, so that the whole earth is sad, and men and animals are greatly afraid, for they love the sun.

Lone Bird Finds Love in the Moon: A Chippewa Myth

The Ojibwa of the Lake Superior region of North America tell this story of a maid and the moon.

There once lived She Eagle and Dawn of the Day along the shores of what white men named Lake Superior. Their only daughter was Lone Bird. Many young braves sought her favor in marriage, but her heart was like ice and she turned them all away. Her father despaired and gave up trying to find a suitable mate.

One spring, Lone Bird went to gather maple sap in birch-bark bowls. She pondered her fate and noted that none of the animals in creation lives alone. She became very sad and sat down upon a rock above the lake to contemplate.

By the time she rose, it was dusk, and the silvery full moon cast a beautiful, shining path across the vast lake. Lone Bird cried out, "Oh, how beautiful you are. If only I had you to love, I would not be lonely." Hearing her cry, the Good Spirit carried her up to the moon.

When she failed to return home, her father looked everywhere for her. At last he looked up to the sky and saw the moon. And there in the moon he saw Lone Bird smiling down, held in the moon's arms.

The Children in the Moon: A Scandinavian Myth

Scandinavian myth attributes the marks on the moon to two children, Hjuki and Bil, who carry between them a pole named Simul and a water pail named Soeg. In one version of the myth, the children were forced by their cruel father to carry water from the well Byrgir all night long. Finally, they were rescued by Mani, the moon god, who placed them in the moon. Another version is told in verse:

Hearken, child, unto a story!
For the moon is in the sky,
and across her shield of silver
See two tiny cloudlets fly.

Watch them closely, mark them sharply,
As across the light they pass:
Seem they not to have the figures
Of a little lad and lass?

See, my child, across their shoulders
Lies a little pole! and lo!
Yonder speck is just the bucket
Swinging softly to and fro.

It is said these little children,
Many and many a summer night,
To a little well far northward
Wandered in the still moonlight.

To the wayside well they trotted,
Filled their little bucket there;
And the moon-man, looking downward
Saw how beautiful they were.

Quoth the man, "How vexed and sulky
Looks the little rosy boy!
But the little handsome maiden
Trips behind him full of joy."

To the well behind the hedgerow
Trot the little lad and maiden;
For the well behind the hedgerow

Now the little pail is laden.

"How they please me! How they tempt me!
Shall I snatch them up tonight?
Snatch them, set them here for ever
In the middle of my light?

"Children, ay, and children's children,
Should behold my babes on high;
And my babes should smile for ever,
Calling others to the sky."

Thus the philosophic moon-man
Muttered many years ago;
Set the babes, with pole and bucket,
To delight the folks below.

Never is the bucket empty
Never are the children old;
Ever when the moon is shining
We the children may behold.

Ever young and ever little!
Ever sweet and ever fair!
When thou art a man, my darling,
Still the children will be there.

Ever young and ever little,
They will smile when thou art old;
When thy locks are thin and silver,
Theirs will still be shining gold.

They will haunt them from their heaven,
Softly beckoning down the gloom;
Smiling in eternal sweetness
On thy cradle, on thy tomb!

It is believed that the myth of Bil and Hjuki may have inspired the English rhyme:

Jack and Jill went up the hill
To fetch a pail of water.
Jack fell down and broke his crown
And Jill came tumbling after.

The Hare in the Moon

Another common image seen in the dark spots on the moon is that of a hare. The hare is visible during the waxing moon, from about the eighth day to full, as a large patch on the western side of the face. Hare-in-the-moon myths exist around the world in such diverse places as Africa, Tibet, Mexico and the Orient. They are most prevalent in the East, and probably originated in India.

In Indian myth, the image is said to be that of Chandra, god of the moon. He carries a hare (*sasa*); thus the moon is called Sasin, or Sasanka, the latter being Sanskrit for "having the marks of a hare."

The Chinese represent the moon by a rabbit pounding rice in a mortar. An ancient story tells of a hare who lived on the surface of the moon and served the genii by making the elixir of life.

An important Buddhist allegory concerns the lunar hare. According to the

tale, a hare, a monkey, a coot and a fox became hermits in the wilderness after swearing to kill no living thing. The god Sakkia decided to try their faith, and appeared before them in the form of a brahmin begging alms. First he approached the monkey, who gave him mangoes. Next he begged the coot, who gave him fish found on the banks of a river. The fox gave him a pot of milk and a dried liguan, a fruit.

But when the brahmin approached the hare, the hare said, "Friend, I eat nothing but grass, which I think is of no use to you." The brahmin replied that if the hare was a true hermit, he would offer himself as food. The hare immediately agreed to do so, and further agreed to the brahmin's request that he jump into a fire so that the brahmin would not have to kill and dress the hare.

The brahmin lit a fire and the hare climbed on top of a rock and jumped. Just before he reached the flames, the brahmin seized him and revealed himself as the god Sakkia. He placed the hare in the moon so that every living thing in the world could see it as the exemplar of self-sacrifice.

A variation of the allegory tells that when Buddha was wandering about the earth in his spiritual quest, he became lost in a wood. A hare approached him and offered itself as food. The hare told Buddha to light a fire. He did, and the hare jumped in. Then Buddha manifested his divine powers and plucked out the hare, placing him in the moon. Still another variation says that Buddha himself once inhabited the body of a hare, and gave himself to feed a starving animal. He was placed in the moon for all to see. Another version says that Buddha, in the form of a hare, gave himself in sacrifice to Sakkia. Sakkia painted a picture of a hare on the moon as an eternal remembrance.

Among the Hottentots of southern, Africa, a lunar hare myth explains the hare-lip birth defect among humans. According to the story, the moon sent a

Throwing Hares at the Moon

Why is the moon dimmer than the sun? According to a Tezcucan myth from early Mexico, the sun and moon originally were equally bright. The gods did not think this was good, so one of them took a hare and threw it into the face of the moon. The resulting dark blotch dimmed the moon's brightness forever.

hare to earth to tell humans that she, the moon, died and rose again, so that mankind could do the same. The hare bungled the message and told humans that the moon died and rose no more, so they would do the same. When the moon found out what the hare had done, she became furious and attempted to split his head open with a hatchet. Her aim fell short and she split his upper lip instead. In return, the wounded hare scratched the face of the moon with his claws, making the dark spots that are visible today.

The Toad in the Moon: A Chinese Myth

The Chinese have another symbol of the moon, in addition to the hare pounding rice in a mortar: a three-legged toad. The myth behind the toad explains the creation of the two great forces of the universe, yin and yang. Yin represents feminine lunar princi-

ples, and yang represents masculine solar principles. Everything in the cosmos is made up of both forces, which are in constant ebb and flow.

The story of the toad in the moon begins in the twelfth year of the reign of the Emperor Yao, or 2346 B.C. Ch'ih-chiang Tzu-yu was a government official in search of the doctrine of immortality. Emperor Yao came upon him one day while walking in the streets. Ch'ih-chiang Tzu-yu told the emperor he was a skilled archer. After he demonstrated his skill, the emperor named him Shen I, "Divine Archer," and appointed him Chief Mechanician of all Works in the Wood.

Amidst numerous adventures in his illustrious service of the emperor, Shen I encountered the goddess or fairy mother Chin Mu, and built her a mountain palace in exchange for a pill of immortality. Chin Mu instructed him not to take the pill until he had completed twelve months of preparatory exercises and diet. Shen I took the pill home, hid it in a rafter and began his preparations. He was interrupted by Emperor Yao, who ordered him away to fight a criminal.

While Shen I was gone, his wife Ch'ang O observed a shaft of white light coming from the rafters and noticed a

Ch'ang O flees to the moon.

Suddenly Ch'ang O felt as if she had wings, and she lifted up in flight. Just then, Shen I returned and demanded to know what was going on.

Frightened, Ch'ang O flew out the window with Shen I in pursuit with his bow. She became the size of a toad and flew up to the moon. There she found a cold world that shone like glass. The only living things were cinnamon trees. She began to cough, and threw up the covering of the pill, which was changed into a rabbit the color of the purest white jade. Ch'ang O drank some dew to remove the bitter taste in her mouth, and then ate some cinnamon. She decided to live on the moon and thus grew to be yin.

To compensate Shen I, the God of the Immortals made him immortal and gave him the Palace of the Sun, and Shen I grew to be yang. The god gave Shen I

wonderful smell permeating every room in the house. She followed the light and found the pill, and immediately ate it.

In Native North American lore,
the dark spots on the moon
portray a frog.

received from the God of the Immortals a lunar talisman that would enable him to visit the moon. Riding a ray of sunlight, he flew to the moon, where he found Ch'ang O alone in her frozen world. She started to run away, thinking he was still angry at her, but he stopped her and assured her he was not angry. He cut down some cinnamon trees and shaped some precious stones, and built the Palace of Great Cold.

From that time on—the forty-ninth year of Yao's reign (2309 B.C.)—Shen I visits Ch'ang O on the fifteenth day of every moon, creating a great brilliance of the full moon with the union of yin and yang. Ch'ang O, however, cannot visit the sun. This one-sided visitation is why the light of the moon comes from the sun, and why the moon changes shape in accordance with the light of the sun and the moon's distance from it.

sarsaparilla cakes to protect him from the heat of the sun.

Shen I grew lonely for his wife and

The Frog in the Moon

Men, women, children, hares, toads—what else is interpreted in the markings on the surface of the moon?

Among Native North Americans, the frog is the most frequently seen image, and numerous legends are woven around Frog in the moon. Frog once swallowed the moon and then in turn was swallowed by her. Frog now sits in the moon's center weaving a basket.

Another Native North American myth says that Frog protects Sun and Moon so that Bear will not swallow them. There are also various versions of the myth of the Frog sisters, who number two or more. The Frog sisters rejected every one of their animal suitors. The suitors wept a flood of tears, and the Frog sisters, to escape, went to the house of the moon and jumped on his face.

Why There Are Fireflies: A Japanese Myth

Once upon a time a woodman and his wife lived on the edge of a forest beneath Mount Fujiyama. They had a comfortable home and a beautiful garden, but no children. One moonlit night, the wife slipped out of the house and prostrated herself before the great mountain with its shining snowcap. She begged Fujiyama to send her a child.

As she prayed, a tiny light appeared high up on the mountain and drifted downward, until it reached the branches of a bamboo. It was a moon-child, sent by the Lady in the Moon. The woodman and his wife were overjoyed.

The moonchild grew up into a beautiful girl, a moon princess, loved dearly by her mortal parents and by all who saw her. The son of the emperor begged for her hand, but the moonchild refused him, saying she was bidden by her true mother, the Lady in the Moon, to return home when she reached twenty years of age.

When the night for her departure arrived, the woodman, his wife and the emperor's son were consumed with grief. The Lady in the Moon sent down a silver beam, and the princess wafted up. All the way, she wept silver tears for those she left behind. As the tears fell, they took wing and floated away everywhere over the land.

Her tears can still be seen on moonlit nights. Some call them fireflies, but those who know the tale know they are the tears of the princess as she searches for those who loved her on earth.

Hina and the First Coconuts: A Polynesian Myth

Hina, whose name means "Moon," was a beautiful maiden who was fond of bathing in a certain pool. One day a huge eel swam past her and touched her. Day after day, the same thing occurred. Then one day the eel revealed itself as a man in disguise: Te Tuna, whose name means "the Eel."

Hina and Te Tuna became lovers. After that, whenever Hina went to bathe, Te Tuna always approached her as a man, but swam away as an eel.

One day he told her that his next visit would be his last forever. This final time, he would come as an eel in a great flood of water. Hina was to cut off his head and bury it.

Te Tuna's last visit arrived, and Hina sorrowfully cut off his head and buried it. She visited the burial spot every day.

67

One day she saw that a green sprout had appeared. It grew into a luxuriant tree that bore the first coconuts on earth. When husked, every nut still shows Te Tuna's eyes and face.

Endymion's Eternal Sleep: Greek Myth

The story of Endymion is famous in classical mythology. Endymion was a shepherd boy—some versions of the story say a king or a hunter—who was blessed with breath-taking beauty.

One night he fell asleep on a mountainside. Selene, the moon goddess, caught sight of him as she rose up in the sky. She was so taken by his beauty that she came down from the sky to kiss him and lay beside him. She decided that no one but her would ever enjoy his beauty, and so she kissed him into eternal sleep.

Endymion never awoke to see Selene. Motionless, he sleeps forever on the mountainside. Night after night, Selene visits him and covers him with kisses. But her sleeping lover brings her no happiness, only pain and many sighs.

The story of Endymion was written in verse by the third-century B.C. Greek poet, Theocritus.

> Endymion the shepherd,
> As his flock he guarded,

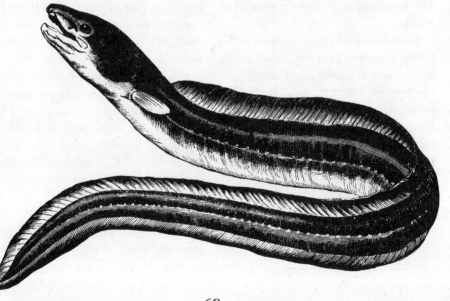

Te Tuna, "the Eel," is the man-eel lover of Hina, "Moon," in the Polynesian myth of the origin of coconuts.

Greek beauty was Endymion's curse, attracting a jealous moon goddess.

She, the Moon, Selene,
Saw him, loved him, sought him,
Coming down from heaven
To the glade on Latmus,
Kissed him, lay beside him.
Blessed is his fortune.
Evermore he slumbers,
Tossing not nor turning,
Endymion the shepherd.

Star Near the Moon: A Native North American Legend

Two boys, one the son of a hunter and one the son of a chief, were close friends. They played often on a hill where they made arrows and shot them for practice.

One night, the hunter's son looked up at the heavens and said, "How small and weak the moon looks tonight." The chief's son was alarmed, for he knew that it is not good to make the moon angry. Sure enough, Moon heard the remark and was insulted. It sent a rainbow down to surround the boys. When the rainbow disappeared, the chief's son saw that his friend had been kidnapped by Moon.

The chief's son began shooting arrows into the sky, trying to hit the star closest to the moon. When all his arrows were gone, he was exhausted and fell asleep.

When he woke up, he saw a ladder of arrows. He climbed them and went up into the clouds. After three days and nights, he reached the top, and fell asleep exhausted again.

He was awakened by a young girl who took him to her grandmother's house, which had been hit by the boy's arrows. The grandmother told him his friend was being held captive in Moon's house next door. She handed him a spruce cone, a rose branch and a rock.

The boy went to Moon's house and untied his friend. To throw Moon off guard, the chief's son placed the spruce cone in the smoke hole of the house, where it would create a wail from the wind rushing through it. The boys ran away.

Moon was not fooled and came rolling after them in a fury. The chief's son tossed the rose branch back over his shoulder. It burst into vines and thorns and caught Moon in a tangle.

Moon freed himself and was madder than ever. He chased the boys. Just as he reached for them, the chief's son threw the rock. It turned into a mountain, and Moon crashed into it head-on.

The boys reached the grandmother's house at last and begged her to help them go home. She told them to lie down and think of the hill where they had played. They fell asleep and awakened on the hill. Their families, who had despaired of ever seeing them again, threw a great feast.

Ever after, whenever they sat on the hill, they sent thanks to the star next to the moon, the house of the grandmother who saved them.

In the Native North American legend, "Star Near the Moon," the young warrior shoots his arrows at the moon in vain after learning that Moon has kidnapped his friend.

> ### The Moon
>
> The moon has a face like the clock in the hall;
> She shines on thieves on the garden wall,
> On streets and fields and harbor quays,
> And birdies asleep in the forks of the trees.
>
> The squalling cat and the squeaking mouse,
> The howling dog by the door of the house,
> The bat that lies in bed at noon,
> All love to be out by the light of the moon.
>
> But all of the things that belong to the day
> Cuddle to sleep to be out of her way;
> And flowers and children close their eyes
> Till up in the morning the sun shall rise.
> —Robert Louis Stevenson

The Dead Moon: An English Folktale

Long ago in Lincolnshire, an area called the Cars was full of deadly bogs. It was foolish to walk through them except on nights when the moon lit the way. On moonless nights, the bogles, dead things and creeping horrors came out and attacked any humans wandering about.

Moon eventually heard what was going on when her back was turned and decided to investigate for herself. One night she wrapped herself in a black, hooded cloak so that only her shining feet were visible. She went down to the bog-lands, where everything was dark and watery and full of quaking mud. She stepped along tussocks of waving grass. Around her, witches rode on cats and will-o'-the-wykes danced with lanterns swinging on their backs. Dead folks rose up out of the dark waters and glared at her with fiery eyes, and slimy hands reached up and grabbed at her.

Moon lost her balance as a stone turned beneath her foot, and she grabbed at a snag. Immediately the snag twisted around her wrists and held her fast like a pair of handcuffs. As she struggled to get free, Moon heard a sad wailing—a man was lost in the bogs. He was running after the will-o'-the-wykes, who led him far from the path while the dead things grabbed at him.

Angry, the Moon struggled harder—so hard that her hood fell back and light streamed out from her golden hair. At once the man was able to see the safe path, and he cried for joy as he escaped. All the evil things fled from Moon's light.

Then Moon's hood fell back, and she was too exhausted to struggle more. The evil things came creeping back and gloated at capturing their enemy, the Moon. They fought all night about how best to kill her. When the first light of dawn came and they had still not de-

**Bogles and creeping horrors
shun the light of the moon.**

cided, they hurriedly pushed her in the water where the dead folks could hold her. They pushed a huge stone over her. Two will-o'-the-wykes were chosen to guard her.

Days and nights passed, and no moon appeared in the sky. The people laid bets, then grew worried as the evil things came closer and closer to their houses at night. Soon everyone was afraid to step out at night, and then they were afraid to turn out the lights and go to sleep, lest the evil things invade their very homes.

The people at last sought out the Wise Woman who lived in the old mill. The Wise Woman looked in the mirror, in the brew pot and in the book but could not divine what had happened to the Moon. She gave the people a charm to keep the evil things at bay: put straw, salt and a button on their doorsteps.

One day as the villagers talked about their plight, a man realized he knew where Moon was. He was the one lost in the bog-lands the night that the Moon had come down from the sky.

The people consulted the Wise Woman again. She instructed them to set out at night for the bogs, with stones in their mouths and hazel twigs in their hands. They were not to speak until they got home, and were to search until they found a coffin, a cross and a candle. That was where Moon would be.

The group set out, terrified. All around them, they could hear the evil things whispering and moaning. At last they found a huge stone that looked like a coffin, and at the head of it was a cross-shaped snag with a tiddy light on it. The group silently repeated the Lord's Prayer and crossed themselves, then crossed themselves backwards to keep away the bogles.

They heaved up the stone, and wonders, the glory of Moon shone out, sending the evil things running for cover. Moon then rose into the sky, and lit the safe path home for her rescuers.

And that is why the Moon shines brightest over the bog-lands, because she knows about all the many evil things hidden there, and she remembers the men who saved her when she was dead and buried.

Moon Rites and Mysteries

The first characteristic that early humankind observed about the moon was its changing shape. The sun appears the same every day and never fails to rise; the moon, on the other hand, grows larger and then smaller, and for three nights in every cycle vanishes completely from the heavens. The apparent death of the moon is not permanent, however, for the moon always resurrects itself.

Early humankind understood that the sun gives life; without it, things perish. But the moon, they believed, *regulates* life. Its cycle has a rhythm that seems to establish and govern the rhythms of all life cycles: the tides, the rain, fertility, women's menstrual cycles, plant life. It represented "becoming" and "being." The moon established a unifying pattern for all living things, living and breathing in harmony, existing in an intricate and ineffable web.

The moon's magical power to regulate life was perceived as early as the Ice Age, long before the discovery of agriculture. The moon was considered an impersonal force or power until about 2600 B.C., when it became personified as the "man in the moon," who, in some beliefs, could incarnate on earth as a king. The man in the moon gave way to gods and goddesses.

Early peoples believed that the moon made all things grow and governed all life-giving moisture. Its changing phases were associated with the coming of rain, as well as with the torrents that produced floods. The moon's fertilizing power governed not only plants and animals, but human beings as well. It was believed that women who slept beneath the rays of the moon would become impregnated by them. Thus, as early humankind developed cosmogonies and mythologies, the deities associated with water, fertility and fecundity were also associated with the moon.

An ancient Mexican stone calendar which kept track of lunar and solar time.

The serpent, shown in an Incan rendition, above, and Mayan rendition, below, is a lunar creature because of its associations with fertility and regeneration.

The Alchemists' Moon

Alchemy is a form of Western mysticism that reached a peak in the late Middle Ages through the Renaissance. Popularly, it is known as the art of transmutation of base metals into silver or gold, which some alchemists, such as France's Nicholas Flamel, claimed to accomplish.

Mystically, alchemy is the transmutation of the soul, the search for immortality, the achievement of enlightenment, the quest for the "philosopher's stone." Transmutation is accomplished through a union of opposites, the feminine/passive/night principle and the masculine/active/day principle. The alchemist represented these opposites symbolically by the moon or the queen and the sun or the king, respectively.

Alchemists veiled their writings, cloaking procedures and wisdom in obscure metaphors and graphic symbols. Supposedly, this was so they would be understood only by other adepts, and their secrets could not fall into the hands of the profane. During the peak of alchemy, between the fourteenth and seventeenth centuries, alchemists produced some two thousand symbolic drawings that survive today. Some are still inscrutable.

The earliest symbols of the moon were the spiral, the lightning bolt and the serpent, all of which are associated with change, regeneration and fertility. The spiral relates to the phases of the moon and to the shell, which is a symbol both of water and of the vulva. By way of association, the pearl became one of the earliest amulets used by women to connect to the moon's powers of fertility. Lightning heralds life-giving rain, which is ruled by the moon. The serpent universally represents regeneration and is the giver of all fertility, to men and to women. Snake—woman relationships abound in mythologies.

Other early symbols were animals who seem to personify the moon because they possess lunar characteristics: the snail, which periodically withdraws into its shell; the frog, a widespread fertility and rain symbol, seen by some peoples as residing in the moon;

The Dangerous Moon

The time around winter solstice, the shortest day of the year, is crucial in the lore of Pueblo Native Americans. The long winter nights are more significant than the long days of summer because the night is the repository of so many psychic fears. The Hopi call this time "Dangerous Moon," and during it nothing grows, the affairs of humankind become unseen, storms darken even the day, and witches are about. Fire ceremonies keep alive the divine light and warmth of the sun.

"**Hermetic conversation,**" by Basil Valentine, 1659, shows alchemists surrounded by various alchemical symbols, including the opposites of sun and moon.

the bear, which disappears and reappears on a seasonal basis; and the bull, a fertility symbol whose horns represent the crescent moon.

The bear, right, and snail, below, are associated with the moon because of their periodic withdrawal from the world. The snail's shell symbolizes water and the vulva, which also are linked to the moon.

Moon-In-The-Water

Moon-in-the-water is a favorite Zen metaphor for human experience. It is used to demonstrate how human experience is created not only by external objects, but also, and equally as much, by the nature of the mind and the structure of the senses.

In the metaphor, water may be seen as subject (mind and senses) and moon as object (external objects). There is no moon-in-the-water if there is no water or if the moon does not rise. Moon-in-the-water happens only when there is water and when the moon rises. However, neither moon nor water waits for the other: the water does not wait to catch the moon's image, and the moon does not wait to cast its rays on water. Moon-in-the-water is created equally by water and the moon.

Thus, experience does not happen to us, but is created by our minds and senses and the external objects perceived by them.

Lunar Deities

A (also Sirdu, Sirrida). Moon goddess of Chaldeans. Depicted as a disk with eight rays.

Annit. Northern Babylonian goddess who was superseded by Ishtar. Originally the ruler of the moon, Annit was portrayed as a disk with eight rays. She and Sin, a male moon god, would come to the aid of mortals.

Arianrod. Welsh moon goddess and one of several children of the mother goddess Don. Her home was in the constellation Corona Borealis.

Artemis. Moon goddess to both the Greeks and the legendary Amazons. Worshippers paid homage to her on nights of the full moon by reveling in the forest under the moon's light. She was associated with the waxing moon.

Artimpaasa. Scythian moon goddess.

Athenesic. Native American moon goddess.

Auchimalgen. Chilean moon goddess who served as protector of the Auracanians.

Britomartis. Originally a Cretan moon goddess, later assimilated by the conquering Greeks. Britomartis would appear in the night sky to aid sea-going navigators.

Candi. The female counterpart to Chandra, ancient Hindu lord of the moon. The two were said to take turns: one month the moon would be Candi, the next Chandra.

Caotlicue. Aztec moon goddess and wife of the sun god. Sometimes called the lunar counterpart to the earth goddess Coatlicue.

Chandra (also Chandraprabha). Hindu lord of the moon, born after his mother swallowed the moon. Chandra is often shown with multiple heads, or holding a hare, which is sacred to him. He was the ancestor of the Chandra-vansa, the lunar race, from which Krishna, the eighth avatar (incarnation) of the god Vishnu, was descended. Chandra is associated with soma, the magical drink of the gods.

Chang-o (also Chang-wo, Heng-E, Heng-O). Chinese moon goddess. According to legend, she was the wife of a famous archer to whom the gods had promised immortality. Chang-o stole her husband's magical potion, drank it, and was forced to escape his wrath by fleeing to the moon in the shape of a frog. She is represented in the dark spots of the moon as a three-legged frog.

Dae-Soon. Korean moon goddess.

Diana. Roman assimilation of the Greek moon goddess Artemis. Diana was often portrayed riding the moon, with a bow in her hands. She was frequently worshipped out in the open so she could look down at her faithful.

Europa. A Cretan goddess who had lunar attributes; her consort animal was a bull. Europe takes its name from her.

Gnatoo. Moon goddess of the Friendly Islands. Her portrayal, as a woman pounding out tapa, is a motif in Polynesian woman-in-the-moon myths.

God D. Mayan god of the moon and

Above: Athenesic, a Native American moon goddess. Below: Diana, Roman moon goddess with her stag consort.

Above: God D, a nameless Mayan god of the moon and night sky. Below: Isis, Egyptian goddess of the moon.

night sky, referred to in ancient manuscripts but given no name. Numerous Mayan "letter gods," as the nameless are called, have been assigned letters by scholar Paul Schell. God D was portrayed as an old man with sunken cheeks, wearing a serpent headdress. He is sometimes identified with Kukulcan, god of mighty speech, or Itzamna, sky god and Mayan cultural hero.

Gwaten. Japanese Buddhist lunar goddess, one of the twelve Buddhist deities, called the Jiu No O, adopted from Hindu mythology. Gwaten is derived from the Hindu god Soma and is portrayed as a woman holding in her right hand a disk symbolizing the moon.

Hanwi. Oglala moon goddess who lived with the sun god Wi. She was tricked by a woman into giving up her seat next to Wi and was shamed. She left Wi's home and went her own way, and as punishment she was forced to give up rulership of dawn and twilight, and to hide her face when near the sun.

Hecate. Greek moon goddess who came out at night carrying a torch and accompanied by dogs. She was said to frequent crossroads, where statues to her were erected. A triple goddess, she was sometimes pictured as having the heads of a dog, a horse and a serpent. Worshippers paid tribute on nights of the full moon by leaving offerings at her statues. As queen of the night, Hecate ruled spirits, ghosts, and infernal creatures such as ghouls. She was the patroness of witchcraft.

Hina (also Ina). Polynesian moon goddess. In Hawaiian mythology, her full name is Hina-hanaia-i-ka-malama, which means "the woman who worked in the moon." Various stories tell how she went there. In one story, she sailed her canoe to the moon. In another, her brother, angered by noise she was making after a night of heavy drinking, threw her into the heavens. In Tahitian and Hawaiian myths, she grew weary of beating out tapa and escaped her drudgery by fleeing to the moon. In another Hawaiian myth, a chief lured her up from a land under the seas, and from her gourd came the moon and the stars. Another myth credits her with creating the first coconuts with Te Tuna, "the Eel."

Huitaca (also Chia). Moon goddess to ancient Chibcha Native Americans, who lived in what is now Columbia. Huitaca was depicted as an owl. Representing the spirit of joy and pleasure, she was constantly at odds with the male Bochica, who stood for hard work and a solemn approach to daily living. In some legends, Huitaca was the wife of Bochica, whom she had tried to ruin by destroying his believers by unleashing a great flood. He took vengeance on her by hurling her into the sky and turning her into the moon.

Ishtar (also Ashdar, Astar, Istar, Istaru). Babylonian goddess who ruled the moon, derived in part from the Sumerian goddess, Inanna. In some accounts Ishtar was the daughter of the moon god Sin and sister of Shamash the sun god. According to legend, on a trip to the underworld to find Tammuz, her dead lover, she had to shed her clothes, which caused the moon to darken. On her return trip, as she regained her clothes, the moon brightened again.

Isis. Egyptian goddess who was both the moon and the mother of the sun. She was depicted holding a papyrus scepter and the ankh, which represents life.

Ix Chel. Mayan goddess of the moon. Ix Chel and the sun were lovers, but because the sun was always jealous, it was a stormy relationship. The sun would routinely tell her to leave heaven, only to set off to find her again. Traveling the night sky, Ix Chel would make herself invisible whenever the sun approached.

Ix-huyne. Mayan moon goddess.

Juno. Roman sky and moon goddess. The appearance of a new moon would bring out her women worshippers.

Khonsu. Egyptian moon god, the son of Amun, god of the air, and Mut, a mother goddess. Khonsu, whose name means "He-who-traverses-(the-sky)," is depicted as a mummified youth holding a crook, a flail and a scepter. On his head are representations of crescent and full moons. As a lunar god, he helped the god Thoth reckon time. Because of his influence, women conceived and multiplied their young. Khonsu was also an important god of healing, and is said to have healed Ptolemy IV of serious illness. Khonsu's principal temple was at Thebes.

Kuu. Finno-Ugric moon god.

Lalal (also Losna, Lucna). Etruscan moon goddess.

Mah. Persian moon goddess, whose light makes plants grow.

Mama Quilla. Incan moon goddess who protected married women. Her most famous temple was erected at Cuzco, seat of the Inca empire. She was portrayed as a silver disk with feminine features. It was said eclipses resulted when Mama Quilla was eaten by a heavenly jaguar.

Mawa. African moon goddess, who ruled the heavens with her twin brother, Lisa.

Metztli. Aztec moon goddess. According to mythology, Metztli would leap into a blazing fire to give birth to the sun in the morning sky.

Pandia. Greek goddess associated with Selene, the Greek goddess of the full moon.

Perse (also Persea, Perseis). Early Greek moon goddess.

Pheraia. Little is known about this Thessalian goddess. Possibly, she was associated with the moon because she was depicted carrying a torch and riding a bull, a lunar animal.

Rabie. Indonesian moon goddess.

Ri (also Re). Phoenician moon goddess.

Sardarnuna. Sumerian goddess of the new moon.

Selene (also Mene, Selena). Greek goddess of the full moon. Wearing wings and a crescent crown, Selene rode in a chariot pulled by two white horses.

Sin. Moon god worshipped by the Assyrians, Babylonians, Sumerians. Sin was the son of Enlil, the storm god; his principal place of worship was at Ur. According to some myths, he begot Shamash the sun god, Ishtar, who ruled the moon and planet Venus, and Nusku, god of fire. Sin was personified as a turbaned

Juno, Roman goddess of the moon and sky.

Khonsu, Egyptian moon god.

81

old man with a long beard the color of lapis lazuli. Every night he rode in his barque, a brilliant crescent moon, across the sky. The crescent grew into a disk that symbolized a crown. The moon was his weapon, and he was the enemy of all evildoers who lurked about at night. Sin also was a god of wisdom and advised other gods. Mount Sinai may have been originally dedicated to him.

Soma. Vedic (Hindu) god of the moon and of soma-juice, the nectar of the gods. Soma was also lord of the stars, plants and Brahmans. He married twenty-seven or thirty-three daughters of Daksha and neglected all but one, causing Daksha to curse him to die of consumption. As he weakened, so did all things below on earth. Daksha mitigated the curse to a monthly waxing and waning. Soma begot a lunar race of kings. The soma drink, a narcotic believed to have divine powers, was offered in rites to the gods and was drunk by the Aryans. Later, only the three highest castes were permitted to drink Soma, and then in religious rites only.

Tapa. Polynesian moon goddess, sometimes known as Hina.

Tecciztecatl. Male form of the Aztec moon goddess Metztli. He was portrayed as an old man carrying a large sea shell on his back.

Teczistecatal. Ancient Mexican moon goddess.

Thoth. A principal lunar god of the Egyptians, worshipped in the form of an ibis. Thoth's origins are obscure. One myth says he was the son of Horus, springing from the forehead of Seth, who was impregnated by swallowing Horus's seed on a lettuce leaf.

An important deity, Thoth had numerous functions. He was god of time-keeping and was often depicted wearing a crescent moon on his head. He invented writing and was scribe and messenger to the gods; he recorded the judgment of the dead. He was the heart and tongue of the great sun god Ra. Most important, he was god of wisdom and magic, and ruled everything concerning the arts and sciences. Thoth authored forty-two books containing all the wisdom in the world; they later became known as the Hermetica. The Greeks identified Thoth with their own god, Hermes; from these two deities came the mythical figure Hermes Trismegistus, or "thrice-great Hermes."

Titania. Epithet for Diana, Roman moon goddess.

Tlazolteotl (also Tlaculteutl). Aztec sex goddess who may have had lunar associations. Tlazolteotl, whose name means "lady of dirt," produced lust and then forgave those who lusted. She especially favored illicit affairs. She had four aspects, which have been interpreted in modern times as representing the four phases of the moon.

Tsuki-Yomi. Japanese Shinto moon god, born when the primeval creator god, Izanagi, washed his right eye. "Tsuki" means "moon," and "Yomi" means "counter of the months"; thus, Tsuki-Yomi is a time-keeping god. At his shrines at Ise and Kadono are mirrors in which the god is said to manifest himself.

Ursula (also Horsel, Orsel). Slavic moon goddess, who was feasted on October 21. Later she became St. Ursula.

Thoth, Egyptian god of the moon, writing, magic and wisdom.

Yellow Woman. Huntress goddess of the Keres, a Pueblo tribe. Yellow Woman is similar to the Romans' Diana and also appears to have lunar associations; her name itself is evocative of moonlight. In myths that seem to explain phases and the moon's occasional daytime appearances, Yellow Woman is killed at night and her brother, Arrow Youth, searches for her with the help of Great Star. Arrow Youth wants her to be alive during the day. He is told by the chief of spirits that she will stay away four days. He is to search for her among melon rinds, symbols of the crescent moon. Then her heart is found, and her head is washed. She puts on a dress and is seen during the day.

Yemanja. Ocean goddess of Brazilian Macumba, Yemanja also has lunar associations. She is portrayed as the crescent moon.

Yohuatlicetl. Moon goddess of ancient Mexicans.

Yolkai Estsan (also Yokaikaiason). Navajo moon goddess. Made from abalone shell, Yolkai was the sister of the sky goddess Estsatlehi.

Zarpandit (also Zerbanit, Zerbanitu, Zerpanitum and Beltis). Babylonian goddess worshipped nightly at the appearance of the moon.

Zirna. Etruscan moon goddess. She was depicted wearing a half moon around her neck.

With the discovery of agriculture and animal husbandry, the lunar cycle became a guide for the planting and harvesting of crops and the slaughtering of animals. The deities overseeing these activities invariably had lunar associations. Deities ascribed healing functions were also associated with the moon, for the moon was perceived to govern all the moisture within the body as well as in the external world. Rites to influence all these aspects of life were addressed (and still are in some societies) to the moon, and to the moon's representatives in the forms of gods and goddesses. For example, in the folk religion of Japan, the *Nijusan-ya-ko* is a lunar fertility and worship rite addressed to *Nijusanya-sama*, the lunar guardian of easy childbirth and good fortune. The rite is performed by women on the twenty-third night after the new moon. The women meet at the village shrine or duty house and remain throughout the night to worship the moon, which appears at dawn the next day.

Because of the moon's apparent rebirth in the sky every month, the moon became, in many cosmogonies, the repository of souls after death. Plutarch, the first-century Greek essayist and biographer, conceived of a lunar way-station for the going and coming of

A lunar crescent, representing fertility and regeneration, sits atop an egg, representing the cosmos.

souls. Human beings had two deaths, he said. One occurred on earth, the domain of Demeter, the goddess of fecundity, when the body was severed from the mind and soul and returned to dust. The soul and psyche then went to the moon, the domain of Persephone, the queen of the underworld, where a second death took place with the separation of the two. The soul returned to the substance of the moon, where it was able to retain the dreams and memories of the life that had been lived. The mind, meanwhile, went to the sun, where it was absorbed and then gave birth to a new soul. In rebirth, the process was reversed: the sun sent mind to the moon, where it was joined with soul, then traveled to earth to join body and be born anew. Similarly, the ancient Indians conceived of a "path of souls" and a "path of gods." As described in the Upanishads, the "path of souls" taken by the unenlightened was to the moon, where the souls would rest and await reincarnation. Those who had freed themselves of the need to reincarnate took the "path of gods" to the sun, which was beyond "becoming."

Deities who have chthonic associations, that is, those who rule the underworld or guide the souls of the dead, also have lunar associations. Hecate and Persephone were two Greek goddesses of the underworld, and Hermes, the Greek messenger god, escorted souls to the underworld. Their consort animals, such as the dog and the serpent, are also lunar.

Dogs are associated with the moon because they are consorts to lunar and underworld deities.

Lunar Calendars

The regular waxing and waning of the moon provided early humankind with its first calendar. The importance of the moon in time-keeping is reflected in the fact that the oldest Indo-Aryan root associated with heavenly bodies is *me*,

Gypsy Moon Worship

Gypsies, a nomadic, dark-complected people with a rich heritage of magic and superstition, have honored the moon since ancient times. Little is known about the origins of gypsies. They migrated from India, perhaps as early as the tenth century, for unknown reasons, and spread throughout Europe, Britain and eventually America. According to one of their own legends, they are cursed to wander the earth forever because of the moon. The story goes that the sun, who originally was a gypsy chief, constantly tries to seduce his sister, the moon, who forever evades him, thus forcing sun, moon and Gypsies to wander.

Evidence exists of extensive moon worship among the gypsies, though the practice has all but vanished in modern times. Gypsies of yore recognized the moon as Alako, a male deity whose powers were greatest at the time of the new moon. Alako was both protector and savior of the gypsy people. In myth, Alako once was Dundra, the son of God. Long ago, when the gypsies still lived in their original homeland, God sent Dundra to earth as a human being to teach humans law. While on earth, Dundra helped the gypsies and became their protector. When he was finished, he ascended to the moon and became Alako. He watches over gypsies and takes their souls to the moon when they die. At some time in the future, Alako will return and lead the gypsies back to their lost homeland.

Alako was worshipped as late as the nineteenth century. Small idols carved of stone show him as a man holding a quill in his right hand and a sword in his left.

Worshippers would gather once a year under a full moon, set up his idols, and offer hymns and prayers to him. The rites were followed by feasting. Alako also was honored in rites of passage: children baptized as Christians were also baptized in his name, and newlyweds were consecrated to him.

Gypsies of Transylvania recognized a Moon-King, the brother of the Sun-King. According to myth, the Sun-King married a beautiful woman with golden hair, and the Moon-King married a beautiful woman with silver hair. Both couples had so many children—the stars—that the cosmos became overcrowded. The Sun-King proposed to his brother that they eat their children to solve the problem. The Moon-King agreed. When the Sun-King ate his children, however, his wife died of shock. Horrified, the Moon-King reneged on his promise, fearful of killing his own wife. The angry Sun-King began chasing the Moon-King and his children around the sky, which he continues to do to this day.

The Moon-King myth also explains the gypsy belief that the moon governs fertility and child-bearing. Rumanian gypsy women who had trouble conceiving made animal sacrifices to the moon by burying two male and two female birds and two male and two female four-footed animals on a mountain in the light of the full moon. Libations were then poured over the graves. Slavic gypsies believed that during full moons, magical plants could be found on certain mountains. The plants gave off a scent which, when inhaled, would cause pregnancy.

which means "moon," and which in Sanskrit is *mami*, "I measure." From the Aryan root descend all words meaning "moon" in Indo-European languages. The deities who ruled time were lunar deities such as Thoth of ancient Egypt, Ariadne the Greek goddess, and the Greek Moerae and the Teutonic Norns, who spin fate. Because time and fate are woven together, weaving and spinning became moon-governed functions as well, with such symbols as the spindle and distaff.

Most lunar calendars were eventually supplanted by the solar Gregorian calendar, whose year is based on the time it takes for the earth to make a complete rotation around the sun. The year of the Gregorian calendar is 365 days, except in leap years, which have 366 days and occur every four years. Each month has 30 or 31 days, except for February, which has 28 days, and 29 days in the leap year.

Some lunar calendars continued to coexist with solar ones. The ancient Maya, for example, had four calendars. The 260-day solar calendar provided the basis of practical time-reckoning. The lunar calendar was calculated on the basis of an incredibly accurate 29.5302 days per lunation, or lunar month. It was ritually important to correlate the lunar and solar calendars, and thus the Maya devised a cycle of 405 lunations, or 11,960 days, which coincided with 46 solar calendar periods.

Lunar calendars are still used in parts of the world, especially by agricultural societies and in the Orient. In some places, the moon is considered to be more important in daily life than the sun. The Islamic year is figured on the moon. Since the lunar cycle is shorter than the solar year, the Islamic new year regresses, beginning earlier each year. The Hebrew calendar also is based on the moon, but it is synchronized with the solar year through the use of leap years, in which an extra month is added to every nineteenth year. Various nomadic tribes around the world use only a lunar calendar.

The Chinese have a calendar that combines lunar and solar years. It has twelve months, or "moons," of twenty-eight to thirty days each; since the moon actually has thirteen cycles during the solar year, the Chinese mesh lunar and solar calendars with the intercalation of extra days on particular months. Even with some months of thirty days each, there are at least five days each year unaccounted for; the cycle of months is begun afresh every

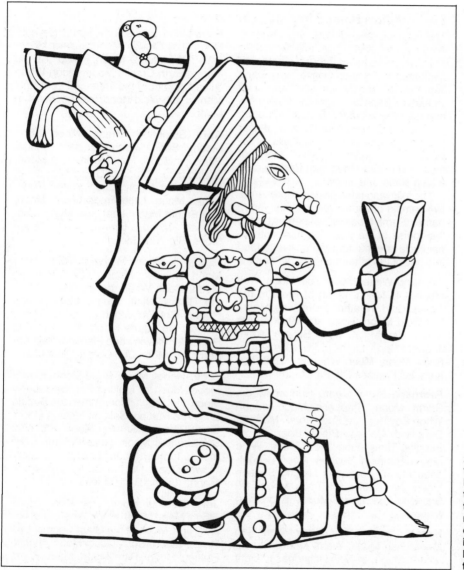

A Mayan scientist sits atop a throne symbolizing the 29-day lunar cycle. Moon symbols in the throne equal the number 20; the bar and dots equal the number 9. This figure, which once graced the steps to the inner doorway of the Temple of Inscriptions at Copán, now is at the British Museum, London.

Lunar Month Names in American Lore

The colonists and settlers who came to America and pushed steadily westward from the seventeenth through nineteenth centuries found that Native Americans kept track of time by both solar and lunar calendars. Each lunar month was given a name for the full moon appearing during the cycle, appropriate for the time of year and reflecting seasonal conditions or activities. The settlers adopted many of those names into their own folklore, and added some of their own.

The following table gives a representative sample of Native and colonial moon names. Some tribes repeat names during the course of the year. The thirteenth lunar cycle is either ignored or overlapped into one of the other moon month names.

January. Winter Moon. Yule Moon. Wolf Moon. Old Moon. Moon of Frost in the Tepee. Cold Weather Moon. Ice Moon. Her Cold Moon. Hoop and Stick Game Moon. Man Moon. Trees Broken Moon. Younger Moon. Limbs of Trees Broken by Snow Moon. Moon When the Little Lizard's Tail Freezes Off. Play Moon.

February. Snow Moon. Hunger Moon. Storm Moon. Trapper's Moon. Moon When Coyotes Are Frightened. Moon of Dark-Red Calves. Black Bear Moon. Budding Time Moon. Elder Moon. Wind Moon. Running Season Moon. Frightened Moon. Raccoon's Rutting Season Moon. No Snows on Trails Moon. No Snow in the Road Moon. Exorcising Moon.

March. Lenten Moon. Crow Moon. Sap Moon. Fish Moon. Worm Moon. Chaste Moon. Moon of Snow-blindness. Light Snow Moon. Flower Time Moon. Seventh Moon. Big Clouds Moon. Lizard Moon. Little Sandstorm Moon. Wind Strong Moon. Earth Cracks Moon. Moon When Juice Drips from the Trees. All Leaf Split Moon. Little Wind Moon. Cactus Blossom Moon.

April. Sprouting Grass Moon. Egg Moon. Seed Moon. Eastern Moon. Planter's Moon. Pink Moon. Fish Moon. Spring Moon. Moon of Grass Appearing. Do Nothing Moon. Deep Water Moon. Ashes Moon. Little Frogs Croak Moon. The Eighth Moon. Leaf Split Moon. Leaf Spread Moon. Grease-wood Fence Moon. Big Wind Moon.

May. Milk Moon. Mother's Moon. Hare Moon. Flower Moon. Corn Planting Moon. Moon When the Ice Goes Out of the Rivers. Ninth Moon. Moon When Horses Get Fat. Moon of the Shedding Ponies. No Name Moon. Moon to Get Ready for Plowing and Planting. Salmonberry Bird Moon. Too Cold to Plant Moon.

June. Honey Moon. Rose Moon. Flower Moon. Moon of Making Fat. Strawberry Moon. Hot Moon. Moon When the Buffalo Bulls Are Rutting. Salmon Fishing Moon. Berry Ripening Season Moon. Ripening Strawberries Moon. Rotten Moon. Corn Moon. Turning Moon. Leaf Dark Moon. Flower Moon. Hoeing Corn Moon. Plant Moon. Turning Back Moon.

July. Thunder Moon. Hay Moon. Buck Moon. Mead Moon. Moon When Cherries Are Ripe. Moon of the Giant Cactus. Sun House Moon. Corn Tassel Moon. Buffalo Rutting Moon. Ripe Moon. Rain Moon.

Trees Broken Moon. Advance in a Body Moon. Whale Moon. Red Salmon Time Moon. Go Home Kachina Moon.

August. Corn Moon. Grain Moon. Dog's Day Moon. Woodcutter's Moon. Sturgeon Moon. Green Corn Moon. Wart Moon. Red Moon. Moon When Cherries Turn Black. Moon of the New Ripened Corn. Blackberry Patches Moon. Collect Food for the Winter Moon. Wheat Cut Moon. No Snow on Trails Moon. All the Elk Call Moon. Autumn Moon. Berries Ripen Even in the Night Moon. Summertime Moon. No Snow in the Road Moon.

September. Harvest Moon. Fruit Moon. Dying Grass Moon. Barley Moon. Moon When the Calves Grow Hair. Cool Moon. Spawning Salmon Time Moon. Ripe Choke Cherries Moon. Leaf Yellow Moon. Spider Web on the Ground at Dawn Moon. All Ripe Moon. Corn in the Milk Moon. Salmon Spawning Moon. Moon without a Name. Moon of the Black Calves. Moon When Plums Are Scarlet. Big Feast Moon. Little Wind Moon.

October. Hunter's Moon. Moon When Water Freezes. Blood Moon. Moon of the Changing Season. Moon When Water Begins to Freeze on the Edge of the Stream. Her′ Leaves Moon. Travel in Canoes Moon. Corn Ripe Moon. Deer Rutting Season Moon. Great Sandstorm Moon. Leaf Fall Moon. Falling River Moon. Falling Leaves Time Moon. Basket Moon. Big Wind Moon.

November. Beaver Moon. Frosty Moon. Snow Moon. Moon of the Falling Leaves. Autumn Time Moon. Killing Deer Moon. Corn Harvest Moon. Every Buck Loses His Horns Moon. All Gathered Moon. Stomach Moon. Snowy Mountains in the Morning Moon. Freezing Moon. Initiate Moon. No Name Moon.

December. The Long Night Moon. Christmas Moon. Christ's Moon. Moon before Yule. Oak Moon. Moon of the Popping Trees. Her Winter Houses Moon. Night Moon. Cold Month Moon. Ashes Fire Moon. Turning Moon. Middle Winter Moon. Big Freezing Moon. Cold Moon.

five solar years. Each "moon" has a name, a central theme and various auspices for human action.

The First Moon heralds the start of spring and is filled with ceremony, renewal of relationships with both the living and the dead, resolutions, and rites for prosperity, fertility, health and longevity. During the first several days, workers take holidays and make offerings, usually of food and drink, to ancestral and household spirits and to Tsai Shen, the god of wealth. The home is purified and exorcised of negative spirits or influences that might cause bad luck. The first ten days of the month each have special significance, such as the birthday of dogs or horses. Around the middle of the month is a great movable feast. On the eighteenth day, offerings are made to the stars. The nineteenth day of the month is the official wedding night of rats, and so humans must retire early. The month closes with fairs.

The Second Moon marks homage to the sun god and earth gods, and is the birthday of the favorite of Chinese deities, Kuan Yin, goddess of mercy and protector of women. The birthdays of Confucius, ancient philosopher and sage, and Lao Tse, author of the *Tao Teh Ching* mystical text, are celebrated.

The Third Moon usually sees the Ch'ing Ming, a movable spring festival during which ancestors are worshipped at gravesites to ensure unbroken lines of descent. In ancient times, this festival may have included orgiastic fertility ceremonies. Third Moon rites also include pilgrimages to various temples, recognition of literary figures, and celebration of the birthday of Wang Mu, the Mother of the Western Heavens.

The Fourth Moon, or Summer Moon, marks the birthday of Gautama Buddha, the founder of Buddhism. Taoists observe rites to honor the Eight Immortals, saints who achieved immortality through Taoism.

The Fifth Moon has a dark aspect, the pestilential moon. The Dragon Boat Festival is held to propitiate water spirits, and other rites honor the god of medicine and the god of exorcism.

The Sixth Moon marks China's rainy season. The rains must come, and if they are late, rites are held to bring them on. Other rites pay homage to Lung Wang, king of dragons, Ma Wang, protector of horses, Niu Wang, guardian of cattle, and Lu Pan, patron of carpenters.

The Seventh Moon, or Autumn Moon, is the Moon of the Hungry Ghosts. The second half of the month is devoted to feeding the hungry ghosts, spirits of the dead who have no descendants to take care of them.

The Eighth Moon is harvest time and is celebrated with theater and entertainment. The eighth day is the moon's birthday.

The Ninth Moon is marked by the birthday of Cheng Huang, a major city god.

The Tenth Moon is Kindly Moon, and opens with a festival of the dead.

The Eleventh Moon is White Moon, the winter solstice, and is considered the best time for weddings and sacrifices to ancestors.

The Twelfth Moon, or Bitter Moon, calls for preparations for the new year. Houses are cleaned and debts are paid. The home is protected against evil spirits with the pasting of gate gods on the doors. A rite to the kitchen god calls

The birthday of the Chinese philosopher Confucius (c. 551–479? B.C.) is celebrated during the Second Moon in China.

for smearing the lips of his effigy with honey and burning it, so that when he ascends to heaven to make his annual report on the family, he will have nothing evil to say.

Festivals and Observances

Even where the moon is not the primary means of keeping time, many peoples observe festivals tied to the new moon and full moon, which are symbolic of beginnings and of fruition. Some African tribes call the moon Pe, the principle of generation, the mother of fecundity and of living things, and the mother and refuge of ghosts. Pe is honored and propitiated in a rite called the "feast of the new moon," held just before the start of the rainy season. Only women may participate (a sun rite is open only to men). To imitate ghosts and moonlight, the women smear themselves with clay and vegetable juices that lighten their skin. They prepare an alcoholic drink made from fermented bananas, and then dance and pray to the moon. They ask the moon to keep away ghosts—the souls of the dead— and to bless the tribe with an abundance of children, game, fish and fruit. When the women are tired, they drink the banana brew.

The full moon generally is regarded as the climax of a month, and various rites are celebrated at this time. Passover falls on the second full moon after the vernal equinox. Easter is always figured as the first Sunday following the full moon after the vernal equinox, and it is used as the reference for calculating all other religious movable feasts during the course of a calendar year.

Ancient Observatories

Another way humankind has marked time according to the moon is by its position in the sky at certain times of the year. Astronomical alignments of both the sun and the moon have been used since ancient times to delineate the seasons and to predict eclipses. It is thought that the "observatories" of ancient peoples may include such megalithic structures as Carnac in Brittany, Callanish in Scotland, and Stonehenge in England, and the medicine wheels of North America.

One of the most studied megalith sites is Stonehenge, located in Wiltshire, southern England. It is a huge stone structure built on the Salisbury Plain over one thousand years before Christ was born. While a host of theories abound about this mysterious—

The Sky Dragon, left, and Sea Dragon, right, are propitiated in rites during China's Sixth Moon festivities.

and to this date inexplicable—creation, a number of scientists believe it may have been designed as a planetarium. Other experts suggest it is a stone calendar for the measurement of the solar year; some, including the National Aeronautics and Space Administration (NASA), believe Stonehenge was built as an observatory for predicting eclipses.

Stonehenge, which is known to have been a cemetery at some point because of animal and human remains uncovered through excavations, was built in three major phases over a period of centuries, beginning around 3100 B.C. Different peoples worked on the design,

sometimes dismantling and reconstructing parts done by earlier peoples. Stonehenge I was probably nothing more than a timber hut in which the dead were left to decompose. Later a henge was built around the hut and cremated dead were buried there. A henge is a circular arrangement of stone or timber, surrounded by a ditch or bank.

In the second phase, circa 2150 to 2000 B.C., ditches were dug, the entrance was broadened and an avenue was created for carrying enormous blocks of bluestone, which probably came from the Prescelly Mountains of South Wales. The bluestone was used to form a stone circle within the henge.

Pyramid of the Moon

Between 200 B.C. and 150 A.D., huge ritual pyramids were constructed in Mexico at Teotihuacan, the "City of the Gods," the birthplace of the myth of the great god and cultural hero, Quetzacoatl. The immense ruins of these pyramids lie about thirty miles from Mexico City. The builders are believed to be the Toltecs.

The city is laid out in geometric precision, probably for ritual purposes. The 3-mile (5-kilometer) Street of the Dead runs past the largest pyramid, the Pyramid of the Sun, which is 217 feet (67 meters) high on a base of 750 square feet (229 square meters). At one end of the street is the Pyramid of the Moon, rising 149 feet (46 meters) high. At the opposite

end is the Citadel, where the Temple of Quetzacoatl lies. Other streets radiate outward, and the city is filled with other religious temples and buildings of commerce.

The exact nature of the rites that took place here is not known. The inhabitants left no inscriptions. They cremated their dead; possibly this rite took place at the Pyramid of the Moon, following a solemn procession down the Street of the Dead.

Teotihuacan went into decline between 650 and 750 A.D., beset by internal strife and savage attacks from barbarians. It was abandoned between 750 and 800 A.D.

According to legend, the bluestone was transported from Ireland and erected magically by Merlin, the famous wizard of Celtic and Arthurian lore. However, it is likely that the bluestone was handled in a more mundane manner, and was transported over land and sea by a slow process that took up to one hundred years to complete.

The final building phase began in about 2100 B.C. and formed the structure that essentially exists today. It originally consisted of five trilithons, each trilithon being made of three blocks: two pillars topped with a lintel. The five trilithons were arranged in a horseshoe formation. By the time Stonehenge was completed, circa 1150 B.C., it featured an outer circle, known as the Sarsen Ring, and a horseshoe of nineteen bluestone blocks raised within the trilithons.

William Stukeley, an eighteenth-century antiquarian and archaeologist, was the first to suggest that Stonehenge may have been used for astronomical observations. Stukeley noticed at one burial site four stones, now known as the Four Stations. Over these stones and another called the Heel Stone, Stukeley found two distinct astronomical alignments with the sun and the moon. The Four Stations have their short sides directed towards the midsummer (solstice) sunrise and their long sides toward the midsummer setting of the moon.

Several subsequent researchers found evidence to support astronomical theories about Stonehenge. Sir Norman Lockyear, a British astronomer at the turn of the twentieth century, determined that Stonehenge was constructed to point to the summer solstice. He also theorized that observations of the stars were made according to stone alignments.

More recently, in the 1960s, the astronomer Gerald Hawkins analyzed by computer 165 alignments of the stones with the sun and moon and concluded that Stonehenge could be used to predict the movements of the sun, moon and stars, and the dates of solar and lunar eclipses. He maintained that the 56 holes that surround Stonehenge, known as the "Aubrey pits" after John Aubrey, a seventeenth-century antiquarian who discovered these ancient cremation sites, served as a counting device to measure celestial events, such as the rise of the moon at winter solstice or the rise of the sun at summer solstice.

Hawkins surmised that the Stonehenge sun—moon alignments made a useful calendar for telling when to plant crops and enabled priests to maintain their power by predicting for the masses the rising and setting of the sun and moon. In 1965, he stated there was no doubt that Stonehenge had been an observatory. It had been constructed to be accurate for about three centuries, he said, after which adjustments would have to be made by shifting alignments among the stones. Hawkins also theorized that Stonehenge was built much more recently and more quickly than commonly believed, between 1900 and 1600 B.C.

Other modern researchers have put forth astronomical theories to explain Stonehenge. John Michell used a computer and gematria to conclude that Stonehenge was a solar temple. Gematria is an ancient Hebrew form of divination in which numerical values are placed on the letters of the Hebrew alphabet. In 1974, Alexander Thom theorized that Stonehenge was an observatory for studying lunar movements, and that it served as a prototype for observatories elsewhere in Britain.

In North America, some believe that the early Plains Native Americans possessed astronomical knowledge and created stone calendars to mark the passage of the lunar month. Large cir-

cles made of stone can still be found at certain locations in the United States and Canada where these Native Americans once lived. Called "medicine wheels" because of their alleged links to religious rituals, they range in diameter from a few feet (meters) to sixty yards (55 meters). The wheels at one time had twenty-eight spokes, supposedly to count the days of the lunar cycle. Often the spokes radiated from a pile of rocks, or a cairn, in the center of the circle.

Although there is virtually no archeological or cultural evidence to support the belief that medicine wheels were based on early astronomical knowledge, investigations begun by astronomer John Eddy in 1972 provide strong evidence for this theory.

Eddy started his examination with one of the most spectacular of the stone circles, the Bighorn Medicine Wheel, located at the ten-thousand-foot (3049 meter) summit of Medicine Mountain in the Bighorn Mountains of Wyoming. The central cairn is ten feet wide and is attached to the perimeter by twenty-eight spokes of stones. The wheel has six more cairns, five outside the perimeter and one inside. Based on analysis of a piece of a tree limb found in one of the cairns, the wheel is esti-

Remains of the Bighorn Medicine Wheel at Medicine Mountain, Wyoming.

mated to be between one hundred and two-hundred-twenty years old.

Eddy determined that the wheel was laid out in lines related to the summer solstice. (During winter it is completely covered by snow and useless as a calen-dar or observatory.) Although he could not find any use for the wheel in de-termining lunar or planetary align-ments—except possibly to count the days of a lunar month—Eddy sug-gested the wheel might have enabled

Mistletoe by Moonlight

Mistletoe is an important plant in the folk magic of Europe and Britain. An evergreen shrub with white berries, it is believed to bestow fertility, healing, luck, and protection against evil. Although mistletoe is perhaps most popularly known as a "kissing charm" at Christmastide, it is still cut as part of folk rituals to observe the summer solstice (June 21) and winter solstice (December 21).

The Celts, who populated Britain and large portions of Europe from about 8000 B.C. to 2000 B.C., regulated all their secular and sacred activities by the phases of the moon. One of their most important rites was the harvest of mistletoe. The Celts deemed mistletoe sacred because it grew on oak trees, the most sacred of trees to them. Mistletoe excited the Celts' wonder because it seemed to be able to grow without touching the earth, and it seemed to propagate itself magically. We know today that mistletoe appears to spring from nothing because its seeds are propagated by bird droppings.

The Druids were the priestly caste of the Celts. Little is known about them, for they left behind no written records. According to the Roman historians who observed them, the Druids considered the phases of the moon before undertaking any activity—including the most sacred rite of harvesting mistletoe for use in fertility rituals. The first-century Roman naturalist, Pliny the Elder, gives us the only detailed account of a Druid ceremony in his description of this rite. The Druids, he said, observed the growth of mistletoe on trees. Six days after a new moon—a time when the Druids probably felt that the moon's increasing powers were right—they dressed in white robes and went into the forest to harvest the mistletoe. They cut the boughs with a golden sickle (most likely gilded bronze), which may have symbolized the sun. The mistletoe was caught in a white cloth as it fell. Any mistletoe that inadvertently reached the ground was believed to lose its magical properties and was discarded.

After the mistletoe was harvested, two white bulls were led to the oaks and were sacrificed. Their throats were slashed while the priests recited incantations for blessings.

It is likely that today's custom of kissing beneath the mistletoe at Christmastide is a remnant of the ancient Druidic fertility rite.

Natives to sight the rise of stars such as Sirius, Aldebaran, and Rigel.

Eddy's investigations of the Moose Mountain Medicine Wheel in southern Canada, displayed dramatic summer solstice alignments. Radiocarbon dating suggests that the wheel might have been in use about the time of Christ.

Witches and the Moon

The moon has long been associated with the powers of witchcraft. The moon rules the night, the time when witches are about; it rules the underworld and the dark powers, which are in the realm of witchcraft; and it regulates the rhythms of life, which, according to universal folklore, witches disturb. The "witching hour" is midnight under a full moon, the moment when all the creatures of the night are at their fullest flower, the moment when witches have their greatest magical power. In ancient Greece, the feared witches of Thessaly were said to draw their power from the moon, which they could command and bring down from the sky. Hecate, the terrible goddess of the dark of the moon and of the underworld, was also the patroness of witchcraft.

The modern West has seen a rise in a religious movement called Witchcraft (with a capital W because it is a recognized religion). Witchcraft is a reconstruction of pagan religious philosophy and rites, combined with a magical craft that emphasizes the use of magic for good. It seeks to dissociate itself from the stereotypes of witches, and to worship, above all, Goddess, or the Divine Feminine. Goddess is represented by the moon, and the moon's influences and cycles play a primary role in Witchcraft rites and beliefs.

Modern Witches see themselves at the forefront of the increasing power of womanhood. They champion the consciousness raising that has led to greater equality of women and men in Western society. They advocate religious recognition of a Divine Mother along with a Divine Father, arguing that without it, the creative power of women is denied. And they work toward a greater environmental consciousness to help earth, the mother of all living things on the planet. Witches believe that recognition of feminine power and influence will help a disaffected society get back in touch with a neglected part of its collective psyche.

Modern Witches say they, too, draw their magical power from the moon, which they usually personify in a triple aspect of goddesses: Artemis/Diana for the young and waxing moon, Selene for the full moon, and Hecate for the waning and dark moon. Magical spells are governed by lunar phases: benefit and increase during the waxing and full moon, banishment and decrease during the waning moon. While both gods and goddesses are recognized as aspects of the supreme being, goddesses, especially those with lunar associations, are recognized the most.

The meeting of a modern Witches' coven is called the "circle," or occasionally the "esbat," and takes place

Modern Witches battle the image of the broom-flying hag of folklore.

Witches brewing up a hailstorm illustrate the title page of Ulrich Molitor's *De lanijs et phitonicis mulieribus*, Cologne, 1489.

One of the major rites in Witchcraft is called "Drawing Down the Moon," named after the Thessalian witches and usually performed at the full moon and at winter solstice. It is a trance ceremony in which the high priestess of a coven invokes and channels Goddess in any or all of her aspects. Goddess is drawn down from the moon, which is associated with female power, fertility and regeneration.

Drawing Down the Moon is performed within a magic circle. The ceremony is begun by the coven's high priest, who alters his state of consciousness through ritual. He touches the high priestess with his magic wand and evokes Goddess to come down into the high priestess. In a state of trance, the high priestess may recite poetry or inspiring wisdom, or the "Charge of the Goddess," a formal address that celebrates the endless cycle of life, death and rebirth, and the existence of the inner strength of Goddess force in every individual.

thirteen times a year, at the full moon when magical forces are considered greatest. Some covens also meet at the new moon, a time of beginnings, for worship and magical rites.

Rhythms of Life

The moon regulates life, or so it has seemed to humankind throughout the ages. Consequently, folklore has organized the routines and rhythms of virtually all aspects of daily life around the wax and wane of the moon. Although science cannot prove the benefit of regulating activity according to the phases of the moon, many people follow the lore, perhaps in the belief that it can't hurt them to do so, and better to be safe than sorry.

Early civilizations based their beliefs about the moon's influence on generation after generation of observation. The moon was believed to control the tides and the moisture in all living things. Thus, when the moon waxed, the moisture on earth below waxed. Plants and animals were believed to be at their juiciest and most active. During the waning moon, living things dried out and slowed down. Early observers noticed that rainfalls mirror the tide cycles, with the heaviest rains occurring just after the new and full moons.

From experience, farmers noticed that certain crops planted during the waxing moon grow faster and more abundantly than crops planted during the waning moon. They came to believe that the seeds benefit from the extra moisture in the earth during the waxing

Many modern farmers still plan tasks according to the phases of the moon.

moon cycle. In regions dependent on peat for fuel, people observed that peat cut during the waxing moon is moist and burns poorly and with more smoke than does peat cut during the waning moon.

Farmers also observed that animals

slaughtered during the waxing moon yield plumper and tastier meat than those slaughtered during the waning moon. They noticed that animals tend to give birth more often during the waxing moon, and the offspring born at those times tend to be healthier. Animals castrated or dehorned during the waning moon bleed less than those treated during the waxing moon. And fishermen found that the best times to go clamming, shrimping and crabbing are at or near the full moon.

One of the earliest writers to formalize observances of the moon's governance over life was Pliny the Elder, the first-century Roman naturalist whose surviving work is *Natural History*, a set of thirty-seven volumes on the nature of the physical universe, anthropology, zoology, botany, geography and mineralogy.

Pliny understood the moon to be central to the rhythms of the earth. "We may certainly conjecture, that the moon is not unjustly regarded as the star of our life," he said. "This it is that replenishes the earth; when she approaches it, she fills all bodies, while, when she recedes, she empties them. From this cause it is that shellfish grow with her increase . . . also, that the blood of man is increased or diminished in proportion to the quantity of her light."

Pliny adhered to the universal belief that growth is enhanced during the waxing moon, and cutting, harvesting and getting rid of things are enhanced during the waning moon. He advised the cutting, gathering and housing of all vegetables during the waning moon. He also recommended the making of seed plots while the moon is above the horizon, and the felling of timber and treading of grapes while the moon is below it. His cure for warts has survived the ages in various forms. Wait until the moon is at least twenty days old, Pliny said, then lie in a footpath with your face up to receive the moon's light and gaze at it. Then rub anything within reach. Variations of this "cure" call for simply rubbing one's hands under the moonlight, or washing one's hands in moonbeams captured in a waterless but well-polished silver basin.

Pliny gathered most of his information second-hand. Among his sources may have been lore attributed to the Druids, whom the Romans said strictly observed the changes of the moon for all activities, such as felling wood, cutting turf, making expeditions and even going into battle. Today *Natural History* is considered useless as science, but it

100

provides an intriguing look at lunar superstitions and folklore that were once accepted as science.

It is not possible to unequivocally deny or confirm a scientific basis for moonlore. Some studies have supported the contention that the lunar cycle influences earth life cycles. In 1930, researcher L. Kolisko found that wheat seeds germinated faster and grew more abundantly when planted at the full moon. His findings were upheld by a later experiment with watercress. More recently, Professor F. Brown at Northwestern University in Chicago found that seedlings absorbed more water at the full moon than at the new, even if they were kept in the dark. Other experimenters have obtained similar results with seeds, and also have shown that laboratory animals tend to be more active at the full moon.

Fish are said to bite on the day the moon changes and the day after.

Plants Ruled By The Moon

Plant	Folk Remedy Uses	Plant	Folk Remedy Uses
camphor	repel unwanted lovers; ward off colds; induce sleep		duce sleep and relaxation; eat to decrease lust
cucumber	cure headaches; enhance fertility	poppy	fertility; prosperity; prophetic dreams
eucalyptus	general healing; green pods for colds and sore throats	sandalwood	air purifier; healing; protection
gardenia	attract lovers	succulents	love and abundance
lettuce	rub juice on forehead to in-	willow	healing; granting wishes; blessings of the moon

Other studies have purported to show that the moon exerts a biological influence through factors such as changes in meteorological conditions, geomagnetism, electromagnetism, extremely low frequency (ELF) electromagnetism, ions, gravity and tidal forces. Critics point to flaws in these studies, citing improper methods and the failure of some researchers to replicate the results of others. In addition, critics point to the great many variables in geophysical conditions and in the individual biological rhythms of living organisms, all of which can influence test results. Thus, scientific proof of a lunar influence remains, at present, beyond reach.

Nonetheless, many people continue to follow the moon for a wide range of activities, including gardening, farming, making plans that depend on certain weather conditions, and even surgery. Scientifically proved or not, they say, the moon seems to influence the success or failure of their efforts.

Lunar Gardening

Guidelines for lunar gardening are simple. The waxing moon occurs between the new moon and full moon, and includes the first and second quarter

Do You Like Your Moon Grass Roasted or Raw?

Moon grass, a starchy root that is a member of the rose family, has served as food and remedy for centuries to the inhabitants of northern Europe, Asia and parts of North America. The plant is a ground-hugging perennial whose roots, according to various descriptions, taste like parsnips, sweet potatoes or chestnuts. The roots are roasted or eaten raw. Moon grass is also called silverweed, for its toothed leaves are silvery on the underside. Bright golden flowers are produced during the summer. The blossoms close at night and on cloudy days. Other names are argentine, goosewort, crampweed and wild tansy.

The genus and species names, *Poten-* *tilla anserina*, tell part of the story of the plant's attributes. *Anserina* is Latin for "of or pertaining to geese," and refers to the appetite geese have for the tasty leaves (hence the popular name "goosewort"). *Potentilla* comes from the Latin term *potens*, meaning "powerful," and refers to the plant's curative powers. Moon grass contains tannin, an astringent, and tea made from the boiled leaves serves as a mouthwash and gargle to relieve toothaches and sore gums. Moon grass tea also relieves menstrual cramps, and a mixture of tea and honey is used to treat sore throats. No scientific data has been published to substantiate moon grass's healing properties.

**Chinese woodcut of crescent
moon over landscape.**

phases. The waning moon occurs between the full moon and new moon, and includes the third and fourth quarters. Generally all activities for growth and increase, especially of plants that produce above the ground, should take place during the waxing moon. Vegetables and fruits intended to be eaten immediately should be gathered at the waxing moon. Cutting, controlling and harvesting for food to be conserved or preserved, as well as planting crops that yield below the ground, should take place during the waning moon. Here is a list of specific activities.

First quarter

—Plant asparagus, artichokes, broccoli, Brussels sprouts, barley, cabbage, cantaloupes, cauliflower, celery, cucumbers, endive, kohlrabi, lettuce, leeks, parsley, spinach, watercress, and other leafy vegetables that produce above ground.
—Plant seeds of herbs, flowering annual plants and roses.

First or second quarter

—Plant grains.
—Sow large areas, including lawns.
—Put down sod.
—Graft plants and trees.
—Cut, transplant and pot rooted cuttings.

—Repot houseplants.
—Pick fruits and vegetables intended for immediate consumption.
—Gather herbs and mushrooms.
—Water plants and compost heap.

Second quarter

—Plant beans, eggplant (aubergine), garlic, leeks, muskmelons, onions (seeds), peas, peppers, pumpkins, shallots, squash, tomatoes, watermelon.
—Plant flowering annual plants and roses.

—Plant raspberries, blackberries and gooseberries.
—Add fertilizer as close to the full moon as possible.
—Harvest grapes for wine as close to the full moon as possible.

—During droughts, plant seeds as close to the full moon as possible.

Third quarter

—Plant crops that produce below the ground, including beets, carrots, parsnips, peanuts, potatoes, onions (sets), radishes, rutabaga and turnips.
—Plant celeriac, chicory, peas, rhubarb, sage, salsify, strawberries, sunflowers, tubers for seed.

—Plant bulbous flowering plants, biennials and perennials.
—Plant trees, including apple, beech, maple, oak, peach, pear and plum, and deciduous trees.
—Spread mulch.

Third or fourth quarter

—Transplant tomatoes.
—Fertilize with potassium.
—Start compost heap, spread and turn compost and organic fertilizer.
—Kill weeds.
—Thin, cut and prune plants.
—Mow lawns.
—Harvest crops requiring long-term storage, such as apples, potatoes and cabbage.
—Harvest flowers and seeds requiring long-term storage.
—Dig herb roots and harvest leaves and bark for use in medicinal herbal teas.
—Dry and can beans.
—Dry herbs, flowers and fruit.
—Cut peat.

Fourth quarter

—Spray fruit trees.
—Cut timber as close to the new moon as possible.

The Moon and Human Fertility

Perhaps one of the most popular beliefs is that the moon influences and regulates the menstrual cycles of women, and thus the cycles of human fertility. Menstrual cycles average twenty-eight to twenty-nine days, roughly the same length as the lunar

Domestic, Health and Personal Matters

A sample of lunar folk advice shows a wide range of superstitions concerning activities from cutting the hair to marrying, to moving, to doing the laundry.

Clothes washed for the first time when the moon is full will not last long.

A stained tablecloth left outdoors on a moonlit night will be whitened by the lunar rays.

Children with whooping cough should drink from cups made from ivorywood trees cut at the correct time of night and phase of the moon.

Weddings carried out during the waxing moon augur happiness and prosperity. The happiest of all marriages are those made and consummated at full moon, especially in June.

Changing residences during the waning moon will bring unhappiness in the new home. For the greatest happiness and prosperity, move when three factors coincide: the moon is waxing, the tide is flowing in and the wind is blowing at your back.

Hair and nails grow more quickly and in better condition if cut during the waxing moon. Hair cut during the waning moon is sure to fall out.

Cut corns during the waning moon.

A robbery committed on the third day of the new moon is doomed to failure.

Childbirth is easier during the waxing moon than during the waning phase.

Babies born during a waxing moon grow quickly.

A child born at the full moon will be strong. If born when the moon is one day old, he will have a long life and be wealthy. A child born in the dark of the moon will not live to puberty: "No moon, no man."

A child weaned from the breast during the waning moon will deteriorate in health.

Do not undertake any business when the moon is in eclipse, lest bad luck and failure befall you.

People cannot die when the moon is rising, unless it has passed full and is on the wane.

cycle. It is said that ovulation occurs most frequently at or near the full moon, and that is why lovers find the full moon so romantic.

The evidence for this contention is mixed. Studies have shown that exposure to light at night—such as from a light bulb—can regulate erratic menstrual cycles. However, an unshaded one-hundred-watt bulb produces light six hundred times more powerful than moonlight. Even if the feeble light of the moon were sufficient to have a regulatory effect, numerous studies have shown that women's menstruation and ovulation are evenly distributed throughout the lunar cycle. So are birth rates.

Weather Auguries

A considerable body of folklore surrounds the moon's apparent influence on changes in the weather. Like gardening and farming lore, beliefs in lunar effects on weather are based on centuries of observation and experience. For example, in ancient times it was held that if a full moon between April 25th and 28th brought serene nights and no wind, then the dew would be heavy, and the crops of grain would suffer. Another belief, recorded in As-

syrian cuneiform records dating to the seventh century B.C., held that "when it thunders on the day of the new moon, the crops will prosper and the market will be steady." In the third century B.C., the Greek physician and poet Aratus explained how to forecast weather according to the phase and color of the moon.

A halo seen round the moon, caused by humidity in the atmosphere, is universally considered to forebode wet weather. This belief has a scientific basis. The radius of the halo varies inversely with the size of the moisture droplets in the air. Thus a large halo means evaporation and clearing skies, while a small halo means growing drops and an increased likelihood of rain or snow.

Another widespread belief is that weather is most likely to change a few days after a full or a new moon. Indeed, studies show that rain is most likely to occur three to five days after a full or new moon, and thunderstorms are most likely to occur two days after a full moon. Hurricanes, typhoons and other violent storms also appear to form more often around the new and full moons.

Weather depends on a great many variables. The moon may not cause certain conditions to exist, but it is theo-

Lunar Weather Lore

Storms subside at the rising or setting of the sun or moon.

When the moon rises red and appears large, with clouds, expect rain in twelve hours.

The moon appearing larger at sunset, and not dim, but luminous, portends fair weather for several days.

Mists under the crescent moon indicate winds. Mists that occur when the moon is doubly convex (waxing or waning gibbous) indicate rain.

If the moon has a halo, rain and wind or snow and wind are coming. The bigger the halo, the nearer the rain or snow. If the moon outshines the halo, bad weather will not come. The open side of the halo tells the quarter from which the wind or rain may be expected.

Moon in a circle predicts a storm; the number of stars in the circle tells the number of days before the storm.

A fog and a small moon bring an easterly wind soon.

The moon scorfs (swallows) the wind.

The full moon eats clouds.

Eclipses of the moon are generally attended by winds but seldom accompanied by rain. The weather following an eclipse of the moon is tempestuous and not to be depended on by the husbandman.

Moonlight nights have the hardest frosts.

Black spots on the moon indicate rain; red spots show wind. Also, a pale moon indicates rain.

When changes of the moon occur in the morning, expect rain.

If the moon changes or is full on a Saturday, it will rain.

If the moon changes on a Sunday, there will be a flood before the month is out.

When the new moon comes in at midnight, or within thirty minutes before or after, the following month will be fine.

If the weather on the sixth day of the moon is the same as that of the fourth day of the moon, that weather will continue during the whole moon.

If the moon changes with the wind in the east, the weather during that moon will be foul.

If a lunar period has been rainy throughout, good weather will follow for several days, followed by another period of rain.

If the moon be fair throughout and rainy at the close, the fair weather will probably return on the fourth or fifth day of the next moon.

If the moon is seen between the scud and broken clouds during a gale, it is expected to cuff away the bad weather.

If the new moon is far north, it will be cold for two weeks; but if far south, it will be warm and dry.

A uniform brightness in the sky at the new moon, or at the fourth rising, presages fair weather for many days. If the sky is uniformly overcast, it denotes rain. If irregularly overcast, wind will come from the quarter where the sky is overcast. But if, without cloud or fog, the brightness of the stars is dulled, rough and serious storms are imminent.

If at her birth, or within the first few days, the lower horn of the moon appears obscure, dark or in any way discolored, there will be foul and stormy weather before the full. If the moon be discolored in the middle of its body, the weather will be stormy about the full. If the upper horn is thus affected, storms will come around the wane.

If the moon is on its back in the third quarter, it is a sign of rain.

If the crescent moon stands upright with a north wind blowing, west winds usually follow, and the month will continue stormy to the end.

If a snowstorm begins when the moon is young, it will cease at moonrise.

Two full moons in a calendar month bring on a flood.

Sailors suspect storms on the fifth day of the moon.

When the moon is near full it never storms.

Threatening clouds, without rain, in old moon, indicate drought.

In the wane of the moon a cloudy morning bodes a fair afternoon.

J. DAVIDSON

rized that its movement around the earth may influence existing conditions. Scientific evidence is inconclusive.

Sailors, farmers, hunters and others, however, have for centuries used moon weather lore to plan their journeys and activities. Their practices, they say, have been borne out by the experiences of countless people before them.

The Moon in Medical Astrology

According to astrology, the positions of sun, moon and planets effect and influence the course of our lives. A person's horoscope enables the astrologer to predict the best times for that person to travel, to make business deals, even to fall in love. Some astrologers suggest that the moon and the stars can help

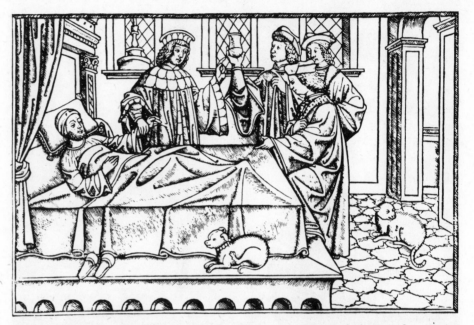

doctors and other health professionals treat and heal their patients.

The signs of the zodiac correspond to different parts of the body. A doctor trained in medical astrology will use a person's horoscope to diagnose or even predict the diseases that are most likely to afflict the patient, and will determine the best treatment as well as the most auspicious time in the lunar cycle for therapies.

Some researchers have shown that people bleed more during the waxing and full moons than at any other time, thus indicating that surgeries might best be performed during the waning moon. Though these findings are refuted by the scientific community, some

Moon in Dentistry

There are good and bad times to visit the dentist as well as the doctor, according to medical astrology lore.

Fillings are best done during the waning moon. Also, look for a fixed sign, such as Taurus, Leo, Scorpio or Aquarius.

Extractions are best done during the waxing moon, and especially when the moon is in Gemini, Virgo, Capricorn and Pisces. Postpone extractions if the moon is in Aries, Cancer, Libra, Taurus, Leo, Scorpio or Aquarius.

doctors schedule their operations accordingly.

Two theories predominate among researchers who have studied apparent links between the moon and bleeding. One, based on ancient beliefs about the moon's regulating powers, suggests that the body's fluids, like the ocean tides, respond to the moon's gravitational pull. The other theory holds that different phases of the moon increase electromagnetic activity, which in turn increases stress to the nervous system and results in a faster heartbeat.

In early times, those trained in the art of blood-letting were told to perform this medical therapy only when the moon was at the proper phase, for the body's fluids were believed to be at a peak during the waxing and full phases and at an ebb during the waning and new moon.

In one of the first modern studies, conducted from 1956 through 1958, Dr. Edson Andrews of Tallahassee, Florida, found that 82 percent of excessive operative bleeding occurred between the first and third quarters of the moon—with peak activity around the full moon. The results so startled him that he threatened to become a witch doctor and operate on dark nights only, saving the moonlit nights for romance.

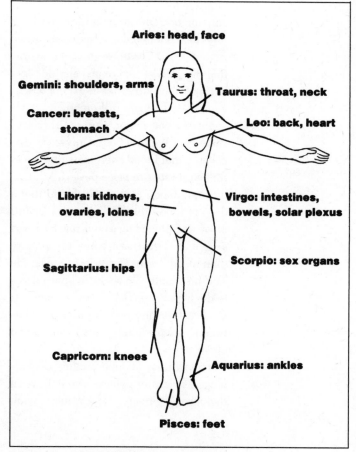

In astrology, bodily functions are influenced by planetary positions in the signs of the zodiac.

Andrews' findings coincide with the folklore belief that the risks of hemorrhaging will be much higher when surgery is done within one week before or

113

after the full moon. A Wisconsin neurosurgeon became so concerned about the bleeding phenomenon that he warned in a 1979 *Milwaukee Journal* article that his fellow surgeons should "not perform any surgeries—except emergencies—during a full moon."

In another major study, Dr. Harry Rounds of Wichita State University discovered that blood chemicals that affect the heart rate are more powerful during different moon cycles. He found that a drop of blood taken after a new or full moon and placed on a cockroach's heart accelerated the insect's heart beat more than blood drawn at different times. He said his results "leave little alternatives to the hypothesis that there is some sort of direct or indirect relationship between lunar movements and blood chemistry."

The validity of such studies is challenged by critics. Those who believe in the moon's effect follow other "moon rules" concerning operations in medical astrology some of which are:

—Do not operate on any part of the body when the moon is in the zodiac sign representing that part. Wait until the moon enters another sign, preferably one that is fixed and governs an area remote from the part to be operated on. Also, the moon should not be in the patient's ascendant.

—Do not operate when the moon is in the patient's sun sign.

—Do not operate when the moon approaches Mars, which increases the risk of inflammation and post-surgery complications.

—Do not amputate when the moon is under the sun's beams and is opposed by Mars.

—Do not operate on the abdomen when the Moon is passing through Virgo, Libra or Scorpio, which rule that area of the body. Instead, wait until the moon is in Sagittarius, Capricorn or Aquarius.

Moon Magic

The ancient Greeks had a powerful magical spell called *diabole*: slandering your enemy to the moon. The spell involved telling the moon about the evils of your enemy and imploring the moon to punish him. According to legend, the magician Pachrates was so successful with *diabole* that the Roman emperor Hadrian doubled his salary. Pachrates is said to have used magic to bring a man to court within one hour, make him ill within two hours and kill him within seven. The same spell caused Hadrian to have important dreams.

Since the earliest recorded history, humankind has looked to the moon as a potent source of magic. Though both sun and moon have been worshipped, more magic is based on the moon. It is easy to see why. The moon rules the night, a world that teems with the unseen and unknown. Its cold and silvery disc sails an irregular path in the sky, waxing, waning, but always presenting the same mysterious face. Its rays seem both benevolent and baleful. The ancients understood that the moon regulates the tides, and therefore concluded that it regulated body fluids and all life cycles as well. The benevolent, waxing moon increased all below, the baleful, waning moon decreased. The earliest calendars were based on lunar, not solar, cycles, and various days of the moon's cycle were declared favorable or unfavorable for a host of activities governing everyday life. The moon's powers were personified in gods and goddesses, and many rituals were designed to propitiate and petition the deities, instruments of the moon.

In Western culture, moon magic evolved along two paths. One was ceremonial magic, a precise art in which the magician follows exact procedures to effect a spell or to command spirits or the forces of nature. Planetary influences—the positions of the sun, moon and planets—are always taken into account in the performing of ceremonial magic. The procedures are spelled out

Astrological symbol for the moon.

A grimoire made of virgin vellum.

Above: A diviner at work. Below: Medieval woodcut portraying Monday, the moon's day, represented by Diana, Roman goddess of the moon, and a lunar crescent in background.

Scrying by the Moon

Scrying is the ancient art of divination by concentrating on a smooth and shiny surface until clairvoyant visions appear. The term "scrying" comes from the English word, "descry," which means "to make out dimly" or "to reveal."

The most familiar image of the scrier is the gypsy woman hunched over a crystal ball. Other ways to scry use the moon or a lunar image. In ancient times, scriers gazed into the still water of a lake or pond at night. Their powers were enhanced if the light of the moon—especially a full moon—fell upon the water. The same procedure is used today.

Unscrupulous scriers used a trick said to have been invented by Pythagoras. They wrote a message in blood on a looking glass in advance, then stood behind their client and turned the glass toward the moon. The client was then invited to read the message on the moon reflected in the mirror as though it were written on the moon itself—a divine revelation.

Modern Witches employ a method similar to gazing at the moon's reflection in still water. They paint the inside of a cauldron black, fill it with water and drop in a silver coin to represent the moon.

English folklore hands down an easy way to scry for learning when you will marry. At a full moon, go to a stream or any body of water and hold a silk square over the water with the moon behind you. The silk will cause several reflections of the moon to be cast on the water. The number of reflections is the number of months before you will marry.

in magical textbooks called "grimoires." Grimoires were at their height of popularity in the seventeenth through nineteenth centuries. Many grimoires written and circulated during this period were purported to be much older, perhaps to enhance their credibility. *The Key of Solomon*, probably the greatest of all grimoires, may be truly ancient. It is attributed to the Biblical King Solomon, who supposedly received from God the wisdom and ability to command an army of demons. *The Key of Solomon* was highly touted during the seventeenth century, but the earliest version of the grimoire may date to the first century, when a book of incantations credited to Solomon appeared.

Grimoires are chiefly used to help the magician to gain wealth and to destroy enemies. Securing love also ranks high in priority. The ritual instructions involve layers and layers of details concerning the magician's clothing and tools, and procedures for purification, casting magic circles, creating talismans and delivering incantations. Any deviation dooms the entire effort to failure.

116

The ceremonial magician pays strict attention to the system of immutable planetary influences that obey natural laws. Magic controls these influences, which in turn control the basic forces underlying all things.

The influence of a celestial body—which in magic and astrology includes the sun and moon as well as the planets—can be captured by a direct petition, such as *diabole*, or by commanding the angel or spirit associated with the planet. In ceremonial magic, the provinces of heaven are governed by seven angels. The province of the moon and everything pertaining to it is ruled by the angel Phul, who has the power to transmute anything into silver, the moon's metal, to cure dropsy and to destroy evil spirits in water.

Another way to capture planetary magic is through the use of things connected to the planet—such as silver or moonstones in the case of the moon—or through a ritual performed on the day or at the hour governed by the planet. Each day and each hour in the day are ruled by different planets. Each planet offers advantages for certain kinds of magical spells.

Monday, ruled by the moon, is a day of peace and happiness. Medieval astrologers proclaimed it one of the week's luckiest days, along with Wednesday, Thursday and Sunday. In terms of magical spells, Monday is auspicious for raising the spirits of the dead, communion with spirits, spells concerning love, emotions and reconciliation, clairvoyance, becoming invisible, discovery of theft, learning the truth, attaining grace, and for all activities concerning water, travel, the sea and shipping, the home and family, agriculture, medicine, cooking and dreams. The other days of the week are ruled as follows.

Sunday: Sun
Tuesday: Mars
Wednesday: Mercury
Thursday: Jupiter
Friday: Venus
Saturday: Saturn

Hourly influences follow a certain order. The ruling planet of the day commands the first hour after sunrise, and the following hours are ruled by planets in the following order: sun, Venus, Mercury, moon, Saturn, Jupiter and Mars. In the course of a week, the moon rules the hours of day and night as follows. (The hours are not clock times, but are counted from the exact time of sunrise, which of course varies according to the season.)

Medieval woodcuts portraying the other six days of week.

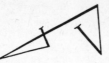

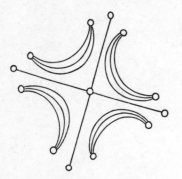

Hours after Sunrise	Hours after Sunset
Sunday: 4, 11	Sunday: 6
Monday: 1, 8	Monday: 3, 10
Tuesday: 5, 12	Tuesday: 7
Wednesday: 2, 9	Wednesday: 4, 11
Thursday: 6	Thurday: 1, 8
Friday: 3, 10	Friday: 5, 12
Saturday: 7	Saturday: 2, 9

In addition to observing planetary influences, a magician always considers the phases of the moon. Spells involving increase, luck, prosperity and gains of any sort should be done only when the moon is waxing, and preferably when the moon is full. Spells of vengeance, discord, hatred, unhappiness and undoing should be done when the moon is on the wane. The darkest of spells, involving death and destruction, should be done during the dark of the moon. This period also is favorable for invisibility spells.

Generally, spells should not be attempted when the moon is new. At the new moon, the moon and sun are in conjunction, that is, they are in the same house of the zodiac or very close, within twelve degrees. This proximity causes the influences of the two bodies to combine and produce unpredictable side effects. Folklore is replete with charms to counteract new moon influences.

Magical tools, which are most effective if crafted by the magician, are made according to ritual and under the proper lunar influences. The tools are

Lunar Talismans

A talisman is a magical object, made according to ritual, that brings about certain desired effects. Each planet has its own talisman, in the form of a disk engraved with numbers and symbols, which helps the magician obtain the magic virtue of the planet. According to a nineteenth-century formula, the talisman of the moon should bear on one side a magic square, a table of numbers arranged in a specific order. On the reverse side are the seals and signs of the moon and of its lunar spirits and intelligences shown at left. If the talisman is engraved on silver during the moon's fortunate aspects—that is, waxing or full—it will make the bearer happy, cheerful and pleasant and will bring security, esteem, health, wealth and freedom from ill will and enmity. If engraved on lead during the waning or dark phases, the talisman will make the bearer unfortunate and unable to work. If the lead talisman is buried, the spot itself will become unfortunate, and anyone who walks over it will become unlucky.

Dr. Faustus gazing at a magical disk in his study.

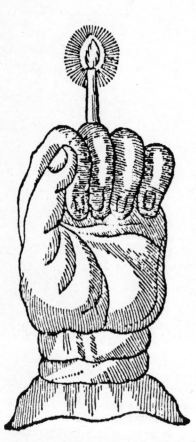

The Terrible Hand of Glory

Grimoires attest to the terrible power of the "hand of glory," a severed and preserved hand of a criminal. Several centuries ago, the hand of glory was reputed to be a favorite tool of robbers and witches in the perpetration of crimes against the innocent. It cannot be said whether or not the hand of glory performed as credited, but belief in it prompted the unscrupulous to try it. The anonymous author of the grimoire *Le Petit Albert,* published in Cologne in 1722, stated, "I own that I have never proved the secret of the Hand of Glory, but I have several times been present when sentence was passed upon various scoundrels who had confessed under torture to having employed the Hand of Glory in robberies committed by them."

The ritual for creating this gruesome tool called for cutting off the right hand of a murderer during an eclipse of the moon. Failing an eclipse—which are few and far between—one could chop off the hand any night while the corpse still hung on the gallows.

The hand was then wrapped in a shroud, squeezed dry of blood and pickled for two weeks in a mixture of saltpeter, salt and peppers. Following that, it was wrapped in vervain, anathema to demons, and dried in an oven or, during August, under the rays of the sun. When dried, the hand was either dipped in wax—the fingers were lit as candles during spells—or was fitted with candles between the fingers.

Thieves were said to light a hand of glory and cast spells to render the sleeping occupants of homes powerless while the house was broken into and plundered. Nothing could extinguish the hand save milk. If the hand refused to burn, the thieves were warned that someone inside the house was awake and immune to the power.

In 1588, two German women accused of witchcraft were said to have used hands of glory to immobilize the victims of their black magic. John Fian, a Scottish schoolmaster who was accused of witchcraft and tried in 1590, confessed to using a hand of glory to break into a church, where he performed a service to the devil. Considering the severity of his torture, the least of which involved the crushing of his legs and the ripping off of his fingernails, Fian's "confession" is suspect. Nonetheless, his case is among those that demonstrate popular belief in the deadly magic of the hand of glory.

All spells reputedly have counterspells, and the hand of glory was no exception. To nullify the hand of glory, homeowners were advised to smear their thresholds with ointments made from the blood of screech owls, the fat of white hens and the bile of black cats.

purified and consecrated—imbued with the will of the magician—under a waxing or full moon.

The wand is the primary magical tool and has an illustrious history. Moses and Aaron used wands to bring the plague to Egypt, and the Greek god Hermes wielded a wand entwined with

snakes as his tool of power, wisdom and healing.

Hazel is the best all-round wood for wands. Ash and rowan also are excellent choices. For spells falling under the influence of the moon, willow is best. Grimoires offer differing instructions for the making of a magical wand. According to one ritual, the wood is best cut at night when the moon is waxing or full, either by an "innocent child," or by a man who walks backwards and reaches between his legs for the branch. The wand must be exactly twenty-two inches long.

Magical tools help the magician tap into the appropriate power. In addition, symbols and fumes are used. The moon is represented by the symbol of a waxing crescent moon. Fumigation—the producing of smoke or vapor—is used to create harmony with the planet that rules the spell being performed. The fumes permeate the atmosphere and bathe ceremonial objects and tools.

Moon fumes can be produced by burning the leaves of vegetables, leaf of myrtle and bay leaf. One nineteenth-century recipe calls for mixing together the dried head of a frog, eyes of a bull, seed of white poppies, frankincense, camphor and either menstrual blood or the blood of a goose.

The complexity of a spell prescribed by the grimoires is exemplified in a spell from the *Grand Grimoire*, which probably was authored in the seventeenth century.

To Cause a Girl to Seek You Out, However Prudent She May Be

Whether in the increase or wane of the Moon, a star must be observed between eleven o'clock and midnight. But before beginning do as follows. Take a virgin parchment. Write thereon her name whose presence you desire. The parchment must be shaped as represented in the figure on the right.

On the other side inscribe these words: Melchidael, Bareschas. Then place your parchment on the earth, with the person's name against the ground. Place your right foot above it, while your left knee is bent to the earth. In this position observe the brightest star in the firmament, holding in the right hand a taper of white wax large enough to last for an hour, and recite the following:

"I salute and conjure you, O beautiful Moon, O beautiful Star, O bright light which I hold in my hand! By the air which I breathe, by the breath which is within me, by the earth which I touch, I conjure you, and by all the names of the spirits who are

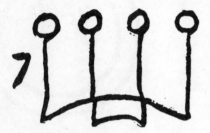

Magical seal of the angel Phul.

princes residing in you; by the ineffable name ON, which hath created all; by thee, O Resplendent Angel Gabriel, together with the Prince Mercury, Michael and Melchidael! I conjure you again by all the divine Names of God, that you send down to obsess, torment and harass the body, spirit, soul and five senses of the nature of N., whose name is written here below, in such a way that she will come unto me and accomplish my will, having no friendship for anyone in the world, but especially for N. So long as she shall be indifferent to me, so shall she endure not, so shall she be obsessed, so suffer, so be tormented. Go then promptly; go, Melchideal, Bareschas, Zazel, Firiel, Malcha, and all those who are without you [sic]. I conjure you by the great living God to accomplish my will, and I, N., do promise to satisfy you duly."

Having thrice pronounced this conjuration, place the taper on the parchment and let it burn. Take the parchment on the morrow, put it in your left shoe, and there leave it until the person for whom you have operated shall come to seek you out. You must specify in the Conjuration the day that you desire her to come, and she will not fail.

Ceremonial magic has always been practiced by a very few dedicated persons such as Pachrates and not by the masses. The second path that moon magic has taken is that of folk spells and charms, simple procedures intended to harness the power of the moon. In earlier times, many such spells were done by the village wizard or witch for paying clients, but spells were practiced widely by individuals—mostly as wishful thinking. Many little charms are still used today. We feel the folk magic tug of the moon, for example, when we see the waxing crescent moon for the first time and reach instinctively into our pockets to finger a silver coin in hopes that the increasing moon will increase our fortune.

Most lunar folk spells call for performing an action or reciting an incantation, or charm at a specific phase of the moon. Remember, waxing moon means increase and waning moon means decrease.

Spells for luck, money, love, good business, good crops—any kind of bounty—supposedly benefit from the graces of the benevolent waxing moon. According to lore, the most important time to cast many such spells is at the very start of the lunar phase cycle, the new moon. But the waxing moon brings new and sometimes unpredictable en-

Why Seven Is a Magical Number

In magical lore and mysticism, all numbers are ascribed certain properties and energies. Seven is a number of great power, a magical number, a lucky number, a number of psychic and mystical powers, of secrecy and the search for inner truth.

The origin of this power lies in the lunar cycle of seven. Each of the moon's four phases lasts about seven days. Life cycles on earth also have phases demarcated by seven. Phul, the angel who rules the moon, is the seventh angel of the heavens and rules over seven provinces.

The Sumerians, who based their calendar on the moon, gave the week seven days and declared the seventh and last day of each week to be uncanny. Furthermore, there are seven years to each stage of human growth, seven colors to the rainbow, seven notes in the musical scale, seven petitions in the Lord's Prayer and seven deadly sins. According to occult lore, diseases run their course in sevens, with the periods of gravest danger coming on the seventh, fourteenth and

twenty-first days. The seventh son of a seventh son is born with formidable magical and psychic powers. The number seven is widely held to be a lucky number, especially in matters of love and money.

ergies into life. Depending on the circumstances under which you first see it, your luck will be good or bad for the next lunar month. Generally, it is lucky if you first see the new moon over your right shoulder, and unlucky to see it over your left shoulder. Better still, see it straight on. It also is unlucky to see the new moon through glass or the boughs of a tree. It is lucky to see the new moon with gold or silver money in your pocket, but unlucky if you are coinless. In the Ozark Mountains of Arkansas, if you happen to glimpse the new moon through the tree tops, you'll get a month of bad luck, especially if you're looking through a closed window. In that case, you'll probably break a dish or a valuable household object before the moon is new again. But take heart—you can nullify the misfortune with a quick spell. Clasp your hands over your heart and say, "Bad luck, vanish!" A folk spell from England for vanquishing the new moon bad luck is to take a coin

from your pocket and immediately spit on both sides of it.

What else is the new moon good for? Spells to increase money are many. It is lucky to finger the silver coins in your pocket, for they will multiply. There are numerous variations of this spell. Most of the following come from the folklore of the British Isles. Some were recorded as early as the eleventh century, but probably are much older in oral lore. Many superstitions were transplanted to America by colonial settlers.

—Have silver money in your pocket. Say, "As you have found us in peace and prosperity, so leave us in grace and mercy."

—Turn the money in your pocket and think about being lucky.

—Shake your pockets and take out all your money and let the rays of the waxing moon shine on it.

—Count your money. It will increase.

—Stand on soft ground. Turn your money over, make a wish and turn round three times.

—On the first day of the first new moon of the new year, put your hand in your pocket, shut your eyes and turn the smallest silver coin in your pocket upside down. This will bring luck and prosperity all year long.

If you don't have any silver coins or money, you might like to try to capture the new moon's good luck in one of these other ways:

—Turn your apron over to the new moon to bring an entire month of good luck.

—Bow three times to the new moon.

—Turn your apron three times to the new moon and a present will arrive before the next new moon. Or, curtsy three times and say with each curtsy, "Welcome, new moon, I hope you bring me a present very soon."

—Make a wish and it will be realized before the year is out.

—If you happen to live in a country ruled by a king, visit him when the moon is one day old and ask for what you want. He will give it to you.

—Upon seeing the new moon, without speaking kiss the first person of the opposite sex you see. You will soon receive a gift.

And, if you happen to make your own bullets, you should wait until a new moon occurs on Friday. According to Ozarks lore, bullets made then will be far luckier and deadlier than those made at any other time.

Children are particularly vulnerable to any unlucky or malevolent forces; according to British and American lore those who see the first light of the new moon shining into a child's room should quickly say a charm to avert any baleful influence of the lunar rays.

I see the moon
The moon sees me
God bless the priest
That christened me

I see the moon
The moon sees me
God bless the moon
God bless me

The new moon is propitious for casting spells concerning love. If you see a dove and the new moon at the same moment, you should immediately recite this verse:

Bright moon, clear moon,
Bright and fair,
Lift up your right foot
There'll be a hair.

Then take off your right shoe and in it you will find a hair belonging to your future husband.

If no dove is about, look at the new moon over your right shoulder and say:

New moon, new moon, do tell me
Who my own true love will be,
The color of his hair, the clothes that
    he will wear,
And the happy day he will wed me.

You'll dream about your husband-to-be that night.

To Avert the Evil Eye

The ancient Egyptians used the Eye of the Sun and the Eye of the Moon to ward off the evil eye, which is literally the look that can kill. The evil eye is much feared in many cultures, even today. Certain individuals allegedly have the power to bring misfortune, illness, disaster and death to those upon whom their gaze lingers. Amulets and gestures are the primary defenses against the evil eye. Dynastic-period Egyptians protected themselves, their possessions, their dwellings and their tombs with the *udjatti,* the "two eyes." The right eye represented the sun and the left the moon. The *udjatti* were fashioned into amulets that were worn and were painted on objects, coffins and structures. Sometimes a single *udjat*

was used, but the amulet was most powerful if both eyes reflected the baleful glance of evildoers.

Another way to divine your true love when you first see the new moon in the new year is to hold your hands across you and say three times:

New moon, new moon, I pray thee
Tell me this night who my true love
    will be.

Then go to bed without speaking anymore, and you will dream of the one you will marry.

Or, you can hold up a new black silk handkerchief between yourself and the new moon and say:

New moon! new moon! I hail thee,
This night my true love for to see:
Not in his best nor worst array,
But his apparel for every day;
That I tomorrow may him ken,
From among all other men.

Go to bed backwards and without speaking, and dream away.

One charm for attracting love requires waiting for a night when the newly risen moon looks red. Then stand pigeon-toed so that your right big toe rests on your left big toe. Make a trumpet of your right hand and recite the following charm three times, blowing through the trumpet at the end of each recital.

Om. I loose my shaft, I loose it and
    the moon clouds over,

I loose it, and the sun
    is extinguished,
I loose it, and the stars burn dim.
But it is not to sun, moon, and stars I
    shoot it,
It is the stalk of the heart of that child
    of the congregation N. (name of
    beloved)
Cluck, cluck. The soul of N. come,
    and walk with me,
Come and sit with me,
Come and sleep and share my pillow,
Cluck, cluck, soul of N.

In English folk magic, the new and waxing harvest moon is considered the best time for young lasses to divine their future. This spell shows how.

When you go to bed, place under your pillow a prayer-book open at the part of the marriage service that says, "with this ring I thee wed." Place on it the following items wrapped in a handkerchief of gauze: a key, a ring, a flower, a sprig of willow, a small heart-cake, a crust of bread and several playing cards, including the ten of clubs, nine of hearts, ace of spades and ace of diamonds. Upon getting into bed, cross your hands and say:

Luna every woman's friend
To me thy goodness condescend;
Let me this night in vision see
Emblems of my destiny.

Your dreams will then reveal your fate. Storms foretell trouble; if the storm ends in a fine calm, then so will your troubles. A dream of a ring or the ace of diamonds portends marriage; bread, an industrious life; cake, a prosperous life; flowers, joy; willow, treachery in love; spades, death; diamonds, money; clubs, a foreign land; hearts, illegitimate children; keys, that you will rise to great trust and power and never know want; birds, that you will have many children; and geese, that you will marry more than once.

The benevolent lunar powers are at their peak on the night the moon is full. If your house is plagued with evil influences, use this spell to eradicate them.

Peel nine lemons with your hands, placing the peels in a bucket of water. Squeeze the peels to release their oils. Visualize the lemon oil cleansing the evil away. Hold this image, and use the lemon wash to scrub your floors, windows and doorknobs. Pour some of the wash down each drain in the house. Repeat every full moon until the evil is gone.

The waning moon is the best time for cursing enemies and especially for getting rid of illnesses. You can ward off any negative lunar spell you think has been cast upon you by performing a spell of protection. Take equal portions of myrrh and white frankincense and crumble them into wine. Shave part of a jet stone into the wine. Fast at night and then drink the mixture for three, nine or twelve mornings. The same spell works as protection against elf magic and any other strange magic.

Lunar Influences in Astrology

The moon plays a major role in natal astrology, one of the most enduring and popular forms of divination since the time of the Greeks. Natal astrology uses the positions of celestial bodies to foretell a person's destiny and to predict events. It is based on ancient beliefs that the earth is a microcosm of the heavens and that celestial bodies exert influences on people and events below.

Astrology began at least 50,000 years ago, when Cro-Magnon man read patterns of stars in the sky and marked seasons by notching bones. Around 3000 B.C., astrology was developed into a system, first by the Chaldeans and then by the Babylonians. One or the other formalized the zodiac, 12 "houses," each 30 degrees wide, that occupy a band of sky, on either side of the ecliptic, the path along which the sun, moon and planets appear to travel.

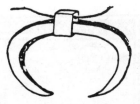

To increase love and fertility, to protect yourself while you travel, or to avert the evil eye, do as the ancient Romans did, and wear as an amulet a crescent moon or any object reminiscent of a crescent moon, such as the claws of a crab, the tusks of a boar or any horns.

Arab astrologer.

ences that act on each of the houses, creating a host of strengths and weaknesses. Horoscope is from the Greek *horaskopos*, "one who observes the hour." The Greeks perfected natal astrology, and their system continues to be used in the West.

The Roman Catholic Church condemned the use of natal astrology, seeing in it a denial of the doctrine of free will. Astrologers were depicted by St. Augustine and many later Christian authorities as being in league with the devil. However, there are examples in popular custom of the influence of astrology on the Church. Signs of the zodiac decorate many medieval churches in Europe.

Astrology reached its peak of importance to science during the Renaissance, when it played a key role in alchemy and medicine. After the Renaissance, astrology declined to a parlor art, though many of today's faithful contend it is a science. Church officials still frown on it.

Astrologers say a horoscope is not predestination, but is a guide to potentials and opportunities. They say, "the stars impel, they do not compel."

Most people who consult horoscopes pay primary attention to their sun signs and rising signs. The sun sign, the

The term "zodiac" was bestowed later by the Greeks and means "circus of animals."

Initially, astrology was used to warn of natural disasters and to regulate matters of state, but by the fifth century B.C., the Chaldeans were applying it to personal destiny. The horoscope, or natal chart, the astrological map of one's life, gradually was born. The position of the sun, moon and planets at the time of birth determines the celestial influ-

house of the zodiac occupied by the sun at the time of birth, determines overall and dominant personality traits. The rising sign, or ascendant, reveals character, abilities, the manner of self-expression, and one's early environment.

However, it is a mistake to overlook the moon sign, the sign of the zodiac occupied by the moon at the time of birth. Since the moon rules the unconscious, the lunar sign influences your emotional makeup, outlook and behavior. It's important to acknowledge your moon sign and pay attention to its influences, astrologers say, for to ignore it may result in the repression of emotions, desires, creative impulses, intuitions and the inner voice.

Unlike the sun, which remains in each house of the zodiac thirty to thirty-one days, the moon changes signs every two to two and a half days. You can determine your moon sign with the help of an ephemeris (a table giving the coordinates of celestial bodies at certain periods) or with astrology books that provide tables. You need to know the date, time and place of your birth. Your exact birth time is essential, as even a few minutes' variance can make the difference between one sign and another. If you don't know your exact birth time,

Horoscope incorporating Christian imagery.

obtain a copy of your birth certificate, which, in some countries such as the United States and Scotland, should have this information.

The following list gives the major influences of the moon birth signs. Bear

Aries   Cancer

Taurus   Leo

Gemini   Virgo

Libra   Capricorn

Scorpio   Aquarius

Sagittarius   Pisces

in mind that the moon, ever sensitive to the vibrations from other planetary bodies, can be influenced by the proximity of other planets at the time of birth. When the moon occupies the same house as the sun, it will intensify sun sign traits; if the moon is in another house, it will temper the sun sign traits.

Aries moon. Leadership and pioneering abilities, determination to be self-sufficient. Protective of family. Easy to anger, and can be impulsive.

Taurus moon. Conservative and stable with a tendency toward longevity. Must have security. Stubborn and tough, but a good nurturer.

Gemini moon. Restless and full of energy, always on the move. Curious and quick-witted. Can be out of touch with emotions. Lack of interest in long-range planning for security.

Cancer moon. Extreme sensitivity, easily wounded. Tendency to feel insecure and to hang onto the past. Home and family very important, a refuge.

Leo moon. Need to be at center of attention. Penchant for grand living. Showmanship can be tempered with dignity. Inability to let others run things.

Virgo moon. Perfectionism, compulsive cleanliness, but well-meaning. Self-doubt. Emotions repressed in favor of sensibleness, productivity.

Libra moon. Selflessness, romanticism. Sense of balance creates good mediation skills. Comfortable with self, but can't be left out or ignored.

Scorpio moon. Intense energy and concentration, bordering on obsession. Secretiveness, tendency to brood. Money-driven, likes to control things.

Sagittarius moon. Dynamic, oriented to expansion and growth. Good teacher, but dislikes being challenged. Enthusiastic, but insensitive.

Capricorn moon. Self-discipline, organization, goal-setting, long-range planning abilities. Practical, material and not emotionally demonstrative.

Aquarius moon. Rebellion against authority. Trend-setting, interest in fads. Intensely independent. Desire for frequent change in environment. Repression of emotions.

Pisces moon: Mystical, spiritual leanings, great creativity. Not interested in the material. Emotional confusion. Compassion can be extreme.

Moon Conjunctions and Happy Marriages

When astrologers examine the horoscopes of two individuals for signs of compatibility, they look closely at the relationships between the positions of the sun, moon and rising signs. A conjunction, the proximity of two celestial bodies, usually in the same sign, can signal harmonies that will help a relationship thrive through the years. If one partner's sun sign is Taurus and the other's moon sign is Taurus, for example, their sun and moon are conjunct, an auspicious combination. Other signs for happy relationships are the conjunction of both moons, and conjunction of the moon and the ascendant (the sign rising above the horizon at the time of birth). It has been an astrological tradition since the time of Ptolemy that one of these conjunctions—sun/moon, moon/moon or moon/ascendant—is required for an enduring marriage. Unless there are astrological peculiarities, these conjunctions indicate a harmonious, complementary balance between the partners.

The great psychiatrist Carl G. Jung (1875–1961), who was interested in astrology—albeit skeptical of its mantic powers—sometimes consulted the horoscopes of his patients in search of clues to their inner selves. He believed that astrology, like alchemy, originates in the collective unconscious, a layer of consciousness, deep below waking thought, whose symbols and yearnings are common to all human beings.

Jung's curiosity was aroused by the ancient traditional astrological and alchemical correspondences to marriage in terms of the three conjunctions. He undertook a study of the horoscopes of 483 married couples, randomly collected, to see how often these conjunctions appeared.

The results showed an unusually high number of all three moon conjunctions. Jung examined the horoscopes in three batches. The first batch of 180 marriages (360 horoscopes) revealed 10.9 percent with sun/moon conjunctions, a probability of 1 in 10,000. The second batch of 220 marriages (440 horoscopes) revealed 10.9 percent of moon/moon conjunctions, another probability of 1 in 10,000. The third batch of 83 marriages (167 horoscopes) revealed 9.6 percent moon/ascendant conjunctions, or a probability of 1 in 3,000.

Marriage is such a complex relationship that one would not expect it to be characterized by any one or several as-

trological configurations, Jung said. He added that the improbability of the high incidence of these three conjunctions in the sample group being due to mere chance was so enormous that it necessitated taking into account the existence of some factor responsible for it. He theorized the horoscopes demonstrated synchronicity, or a "meaningful coincidence."

Somehow, persons who were compatible according to their horoscopes had found each other and married. (However, Jung offered no comment upon the happiness or stability of the marriages in his astrological study.)

Although the results appeared to validate astrology, Jung said they did not. In his monograph, *Synchronicity: An Acausal Connecting Principle* (1960), he opined that the astrological correspondences simply existed "like any other agreeable or annoying accident, and it seems doubtful to me whether it can be proved scientifically to be anything more than that."

Nonetheless, the incidence of the lunar conjunctions in the marital horoscopes remains intriguing. Does the moon really influence our choices in marriage in a subtle, subconscious way? Believers continue to say yes, and skeptics say no.

Daily Lunar Auspices

The moon leaves one sign, or house, of the zodiac and enters another one every two to two and a half days. In each sign, the moon exerts unique influences on the processes of the unconscious, thus affecting certain undertakings. The influences wax and wane as the moon enters each sign and takes its leave, and are tempered by the moon's phase and the signs on either side.

When the moon is in transit, that is, at the end of a sign or just entering a sign, it is "void of course," and such a period is particularly fraught with uncertainties. The distance the moon traverses in any given day is called a mansion of the moon. (This is not to be confused with the twelve houses of the zodiac.) The first mansion begins at 0 degrees Aries, the second mansion at about 12 or 13 degrees Aries, and so on. Each mansion has its influences as well.

Thanks to the moon, every day of the month has favorable or unfavorable aspects for some activity. To find out auspices, you'll need an ephemeris to determine the moon's location at a given day and hour.

The general lunar auspices within a

Beware When the Moon Goes Void of Course

When the moon departs from one sign of the zodiac and enters into the next it is void of course, and the transition is a tricky little time. The moon exerts a certain influence while it occupies a sign, but in transit it has nothing to affect. And so, it seems, the moon does not quite know what to do.

As a result, life below on earth can turn topsy turvy. Decisions made when the moon is void of course go sour. Newly purchased objects break, are defective or are left unused. Agreements made that seemed rock-solid change later. Moon void of course is a time when crazy and odd things happen, behavior is erratic, objects are misplaced, mistakes are made and we lose our way. Those who are accident-prone are likely to have a mishap. Travel is subject to delays, cancellations and accidents.

Astrologers differ as to how significant the void-of-course influence is, but most at least advise caution during these times. If possible, stick to routine matters and projects already underway. Avoid launching new projects, signing contracts, making major decisions (especially financial ones) and traveling.

The moon goes void of course roughly every two to two and a half days. Some void periods last only for a few minutes, but most last several hours, and some for a day or more. They can be calculated with the help of an ephemeris. You can make up a void-of-course calendar months in advance to help you plan your time.

particular sign of the zodiac are as follows.

Moon in Aries. A time geared to action, enthusiasm, risk-taking, aggression and independent decision-making. Things move quickly, but the energy is short-lived. Watch out for impulsiveness.

Moon in Taurus. The solid and patient Taurean bull yields caution, reserve, practicality and protection of interests. A poor time for making changes, especially financial. Enter-prises begun now have lasting value but will be hard to change.

Moon in Gemini. A highly changeable, fickle state. Avoid beginning new projects and concentrate on communication and exchange of ideas and wit. Playfulness is in the air. A good time for meetings and being with family.

Moon in Cancer. The moon is in its own house here, and sensitivities and emotions run high. Avoid stepping on toes. People who tend to be gullible need to be extra careful. It is easy to

Astrological sign for Cancer.

Cancer: The Moon's Own Child

Of the twelve signs of the zodiac, Cancer is the one ruled by the moon. Cancerians, or Moon Children, as they also are called, reflect lunar influences more than any other sign. They are deeply in touch with their emotions and intuitions, are introverted, shy and somewhat mysterious. It is often difficult for others to plumb and understand the full measure of their emotional depth. They are tenacious and loyal once they feel secure, but also are prone to moodiness and are easy to slight. When wounded, the Cancerian scuttles for cover and can remain in a funk for days. A marriage between two Cancerians courts disaster, for after a spat the partners may retreat wounded into their own silent worlds, waiting to be coaxed out. Their ideal partners are their zodiac opposite, the Capricorn goats, whose practical sensibilities help keep Cancerians grounded.

Home is very important to Cancerians—they must have a place where they can feel protected from buffeting by the external world. They are interested in domestic activities and tend to make good parents and good cooks, although at times their emotionalism can be smothering. Because they are in tune with their inner selves, they tend to be very creative, and make excellent writers and artists.

overindulge in food, drink and moodiness.

Moon in Leo. Entertainment, showmanship and vitality reign. Take center stage, express yourself. Great opportunities to make good impressions and sell ideas, but don't go overboard.

Moon in Virgo. Emphasis on details, organization, concentration, routine tasks, research. A good time for intellectual matters, shopping for bargains and attending to health.

Moon in Libra. Charm, eloquence and artistic expression come to the fore. Good time for new friendships, romance, marriage and partnerships. Give time to yourself. Avoid emotional conflicts.

Moon in Scorpio. People are likely to be critical and suspicious, especially concerning money matters. Heightened emotional sensitivity can lead to anger and malice. Habits, family loyalties strong.

Moon in Sagittarius. Honesty, optimism and imagination open up. Emphasis on intellectual, philosophical thought. Take a trip, have an adventure, break routine.

Moon in Capricorn. The establishment, authority, rules and regulations are staunchly upheld. Practicality prevails, but progress can seem fraught with obstacles. A tendency toward depression, pessimism and frustration. Good time for discipline and hard work.

Moon in Aquarius. Social activities and concerns and rational thought prevail. Good time for new ideas, planning the future. Excessive emphasis on ideals can bring disappointment.

Moon in Pisces. There are urges to confide and seek advice, but confusion makes manipulation of others possible. Interest in the spiritual, a good time for oracles. Energies turn inward.

The Moon in Palmistry

Palmistry is closely allied with astrology. This method of divination is based on the shape of the hands and the lines and mounds on the palms and fingers. It is one of the oldest forms of divination, believed to have originated in China or India as early as 3000 B.C. It is also known as cheiromancy or chiromancy, named after Cheiro, a popular Irish fortuneteller.

Palmistry assigns the signs of the zodiac, and the sun, moon and planets to locations on the hand. Each governs an aspect of life, such as longevity, health,

love, career or money. A palmist first looks at the shape of the hands, which indicates physical or artistic activities. The palmist then observes the lines, fingers, fleshy mounts, and flexibility. The left hand carries the imprint of destiny at birth, while the right is a map of how that destiny has or has not been carried out. If a person is left-handed, the roles of the hands are reversed.

The five major lines are: the line of life, which rules longevity and stages in life; the line of the heart, emotions and intuition; the line of the head, the intellect; the line of Saturn, good fortune; the hepatica line, health. In addition, marriage lines are on the outer palm, and numerous other small lines yield more details about you.

Mounts are fleshy portions, and each mount reveals an aspect of personality. For example, a well-developed mount of Venus, at the base of the thumb, indicates compassion and warmth.

The mount of the moon is located on the outer palm. If the area bulges and is exceptionally fleshy, the individual is marked as a "lunarian," someone with great imagination, artistic ability and psychic gifts. According to palmistry lore, lunarians are restless, romantic, emotional and superstitious. They are sensitive to infections, nervous disor-

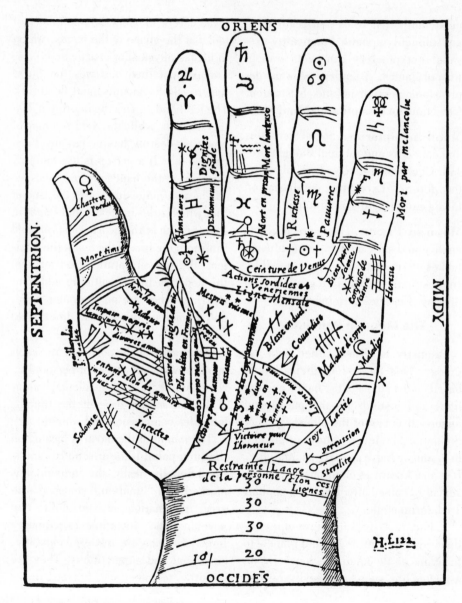

The hand's shape and lines reveal personality and destiny, according to palmistry. The mount of the moon is marked by a crescent on the outer palm.

ders, and problems with the kidneys, gall bladder and lower intestines. Extreme types may be prone to irrationality and even lunacy. If the mount of the moon is poorly developed, the individual lacks imagination and is not a lunarian.

Markings within the mount of the moon reveal details. If a small, star-shaped marking of lines appears, the individual possesses imagination of such degree as to be either genius or lunatic. Triangular markings reveal the hand of a superb writer of fiction. Cross-hatched areas, or grills as they are called in palmistry, show that the

---

Her Palm Foretold Her Glory and Her Fate

Lunar aspects in the left hand of Empress Josephine Bonaparte foretold that she would "enjoy boundless glory, have two husbands, amaze the world by her portentous fortune, and sadden her friends by her grievous and premature end," according to her palmist, Mme M. A. Le Normand. Her destiny was, for the most part, fulfilled.

Josephine, born Marie Josèphe Rose Tascher de la Pagerie on June 23, 1763, was a comely but unsophisticated girl who aspired to the glittering courts of high society. In 1779, she married Alexandre, vicomte de Beauharnais, and bore him a son and a daughter. He lost his head to the guillotine in 1794 for his role in the Revolution.

Josephine, by then quite sophisticated, caught the eye of Napoleon Bonaparte, a rising young general, whom she wed in a civil ceremony on March 9, 1796. He was madly in love with her, but she considered him primarily an entree to the society she desired. During his Egyptian campaign from 1798–99, she ignored his passionate love letters and amused herself by having an affair and running up stupendous debts with her lavish entertaining. The furious Napoleon threatened to divorce her, then relented.

After he became emperor, Josephine persuaded him to marry her in a religious ceremony on December 1, 1804. But her coolness, and her inability to bear him a son, led Napoleon to seek nullification of the marriage on a technicality—the absence of a parish priest at the religious ceremony. The marriage ended on December 14, 1809.

Napoleon then wed Marie-Louise, daughter of Emperor Francis I of Austria. Josephine, out of the limelight, retired to her private residence at Malmaison outside of Paris. She continued to throw lavish parties, however, and Napoleon continued to pay for them, perhaps out of guilt.

Soon after Napoleon's abdication in 1814, Josephine died quietly at Malmaison. She was fifty, a respectable age for the times and certainly not an age of premature death, but her life ended in faded glory. Alas, if she had only paid attention to her palm. Josephine's left palm is shown at right.

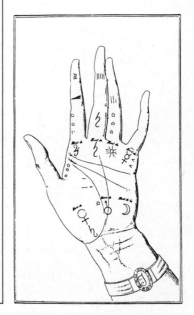

---

individual is constantly discontent and always seeks to be somewhere else.

Take a look at your palm now and see what the moon has to say about you.

The Moon in the Tarot

The Tarot, a deck of seventy-eight cards, has been a popular system of divination since the eighteenth century. The name is a French derivative of the Italian *tarocchi*, meaning "triumphs" or "trumps." The exact origins of the Tarot are unknown. Some occultists have suggested that the cards are of great antiquity, the remnants of the fabled esoteric teachings of Hermes Trismegistus, the legendary Greco-Egyptian figure who gave humankind all its learning. More likely, the cards evolved out of the many decks of playing cards which spread throughout Europe as early as the fourteenth century.

The Tarot is divided into two parts, the Major Arcana, or trumps, comprising twenty-two cards, and the Minor Arcana, comprising fifty-six cards. The Major Arcana present images that mirror truths and stages of enlightenment in the soul's journey toward wholeness. The Minor Arcana are divided into four suits of fourteen cards each and resemble today's playing cards.

THE MOON .

Each Tarot card—particularly of the Major Arcana—is heavy with symbolism, which is interpreted for divination. For readings, Tarot cards are shuffled and laid out in various spreads. Each position in a spread has a particular significance. The meaning of the card also depends on whether it falls upright or reversed (upside down). Though each card and its position has a unique meaning, the entire layout must be considered synergistically.

Ideally, the Tarot is not consulted for "yes" or "no" answers, but for insight into situations and forces in motion. Skillful reading requires good intuition, an ability governed by the moon herself. Besides divination, the Tarot is used in meditation and creative visualization exercises as a means of personal growth.

Lunar symbols representing the unconscious, intuition, creativity, emotions and the nurturing forces of nature are threaded throughout the deck, but are most dramatic in two Major Arcana, The High Priestess, which bears the number II, and The Moon, which bears the number XVIII. Here is what those cards symbolize.

II The High Priestess. The High Priestess is a lunar emissary, bringing

THE HIGH PRIESTESS

the powerful forces of the unconscious into waking life. The great fertilizing, nourishing energies of nature emanate from her. Like the moon, represented by the crescent at her feet, the High Priestess reveals little about herself. She appears tranquil and all-knowing, yet the source of her knowledge is kept hidden like the dark side of the moon. Her silence exudes confidence and mystery. She gives us part of the answer we seek, and her lunar glow encourages us to meditate and listen to the intuitive voice within. The rest of the answer will come when we are ready.

Reversed: You are ignoring your emotions and intuition. Your heart tells you what is right, yet you seek external validation. Learn to follow your hunches.

XVIII The Moon. The Moon symbolizes a netherworld of dreams and illusions, as intangible as the light cast by the moon herself. When the moon rides high in the night sky, her silvery glow creates a dreamworld in which familiar shapes take on strange twists and shadows, and things are not as they seem. The moon steers its own course, changing shape and going to an unknown destination. The traveler through the lunar world must be on guard.

The Moon card suggests we are being tested. Can we remain true to the path, or will we be distracted by the shadows and illusions? Will we be able to tell dream from reality, and more importantly, will we be able to glean from dreams what needs to be applied to reality? The Moon indicates that to pass the test, we must learn to trust our inner voice and intuition, our unconscious self. The lunar rays pull us onward.

Reversed: This is not a time to venture out—you lack faith in yourself. You're going through a dark phase, so stay with the path you know best until things brighten.

The lunar aspects and essence of The High Priestess and The Moon can be drawn upon in meditation for personal growth and awareness. To meditate on the cards, select a time when you can relax and be quiet and uninterrupted for a while. Sit comfortably—if you lie down you may fall asleep—and take the High Priestess and the Moon cards out of the Tarot deck. You can either fix an image of them in your mind with your eyes closed, or gaze at them. Drink in the images, the details, the symbols and their meanings. Think about how the cards apply to yourself and your own life. Act out dramas within the cards. Become the High Priestess or carry on a conversation with her. Stand beneath the Moon and listen to the dogs and wolves howl. Let your thoughts flow freely. When you are done meditating, write down your thoughts in a journal so that you remember them and can refer to and reflect on them later.

Here are some thoughts to help you get started.

II The High Priestess. The symbol of life-giving forces, the creative force and the unseen in nature, the High Priestess communicates without speaking and conveys tranquility. She penetrates barriers and disguises to see things as they really are. She teaches us that we are connected to everything else. Thus, try becoming one with nature: blend into a river, become part of a tree. Realize that you advance and grow in life by fully becoming part of everything around you, not by standing on the sidelines as an observer. Learn to listen to your inner voice.

XVIII The Moon. The Moon lights an inner path, one filled with shadows and shapes and illusions. Here we confront our deepest and most hidden fears and our self-doubts. What are they? Can you give them shapes and names? In so doing, see how they can be overcome. Perhaps they are not as real as you thought. What is your subconscious trying to communicate to you? Trust your instincts.

Moon Madness and Night Things

The universe is comprised of opposites: light and dark, hot and cold, good and evil, life and death, love and hate, male and female. These opposites push and pull in an unending cycle of birth, growth, decay, death and rebirth.

The moon, too, is ascribed opposing powers and traits. In its benevolent aspect, it has been perceived through the millennia as regulating life and stimulating things to grow. In its malevolent aspect, the moon destroys.

Since ancient times, people have believed that the moon has the power to bring on madness, seizures, suicide and heinous crimes. People have also believed that, in its baleful aspect, the moon gives strength and power to the evil spirits and creatures who rule the night.

Many of these beliefs are the stuff of folklore—like the notion that sleeping in the moonlight will drive you insane, or that a full moon, combined with a curse or potion, will transform a human into a werewolf.

But not all appears to be fancy. Under full moons the numbers of homicides and suicides are said to climb. Lycanthropy, the delusion of thinking oneself to be a werewolf, does exist and cases have been recorded in modern medical history.

The extent of the moon's actual influence is not known for certain. Some scientists caution against giving any credence to what they term "lunar effects," while others say that evidence strongly suggests that the moon does affect human affairs.

Fact or fancy, plenty of people in modern times believe that the moon is a tremendously powerful and sometimes malevolent force. While no one knows absolutely if it is or is not so about the moon, one thing is certain: as long as the moon continues to shine, the search for answers will continue.

Driven Mad by the Moon

For centuries, the moon has been blamed for strange and abnormal behavior—even insanity. The word "lunacy," for instance, is derived from the Latin word, *luna*, for moon. From "lunacy" we get the popular "loony."

Many early superstitions warned of the mentally disruptive dangers of exposure to moonlight. Pregnant women were told that if they went out when the moon was full they would give birth to lunatics. Passages in the Talmud and the Old and New Testaments attribute lunacy to the effects of the moon.

According to an old Irish superstition, sleeping with the moon shining on the face produces a form of blindness and a state of harmless idiocy called "moonstruck."

Early medicine helped forge the first supposed physiological links between the moon and insanity. Roman physicians advanced the notion that moonlight increased moisture in the air, causing brain seizures.

The sixteenth-century physician, Paracelsus, said that the moon had the "power to tear reason out of man's head by depriving him of humors and cerebral virtues." The moon, he added, was most powerful when full.

In the Middle Ages, the Catholic Church attacked superstitions that credited the moon with awesome powers. In a failed attempt to rid people of their pagan beliefs, the Church argued that the moon itself did not cause madness. Rather, said the Church, it was the devil acting on the moon that turned people insane. During the Inquisition of the late Middle Ages and Renaissance, Church inquisitors allowed that celestial bodies could influence devils, who would in turn harass human beings. The *Malleus Maleficarum* (1486), written by two Dominicans, Heinrich Kramer and James Sprenger, became a handbook for witch-hunting. It stated, "The stars can influence the devils themselves. [As proof of this] certain men who are called lunatics are molested by devils more at one time than at another; and the devils ... would rather molest them at all times, unless they themselves were deeply affected by certain phases of the Moon."

Eventually, links between the moon and madness—the changing phases of the moon, in particular—took root in English law. Sir William Hale, who later became chief justice of England, wrote in the 1600s, "The moon hath a great influence in all diseases of the brain . . . especially dementia; such persons commonly in the full and change of the moon, especially about the equinoxes and summer solstice, are usually at the height of their distemper."

Moon madness became accepted as fact. "When the moon is on the full, or new, people are more irritable than at other times. . . . Insanity at these times has its worst paroxysms," intoned T. F. Forster in the *Pocket Encyclopedia* in 1827. Each full moon was believed to worsen the symptoms of madness.

The distinguished eighteenth-century English jurist, Sir William Blackstone, later described a lunatic as someone who would "lose" or "enjoy" his reason, "depending on the changes of the moon." England's Lunacy Act of 1842 used similar logic. A lunatic was someone who was lucid during the two weeks prior to a full moon but who acted strangely during the following fourteen days. As late as 1940, an English soldier charged with murdering his comrade pleaded "moon madness" as his defense at Winchester Assizes. He said the madness overcame him each full moon.

Many modern researchers were influenced by the writings of Dr. Benjamin Rush, one of the signers of the American Declaration of Independence. In his *Medical Inquiries and Observations upon Diseases of the Mind*, he wrote that "the moon, when full increases the rarity of air and the quantity of light, each of which acts upon people with various diseases, and among others, in madness."

Following Rush's work, researchers over the years advanced a range of other

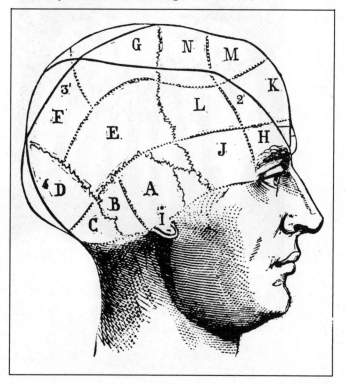

143

"moon madness" theories. Some suggested that the moon's gravitational pull was a cause of insanity, while as late as the 1960s one scientist tried to draw parallels between changes to the brain's electrical charges and the rhythms of the lunar cycles.

According to one study, virtually no evidence connects the moon with mental illness. Supposed increases in hospital admissions and related aberrant behavior due to the result of full moons were dismissed in a 1985 study by James Rotton and I. W. Kelly. The authors, who reviewed thirty-five prior studies on the topic, concluded that "the phases of the moon accounted for no more than one percent of the variance in activities termed lunacy."

Superstitions die hard, however. In 1987, a farmer in Devon, England, was quoted as saying he believed that the moon controls all fluids within the body, including those in the brain: "I know a matron of a home for the elderly, she's Jewish by the way, in East London, who marked the full moon on the calendar to warn the staff. The patients always went slightly crazy at the full moon, she said." And in parts of Yorkshire, people still say that those who seem a bit strange or unstable in character are "ruled by t'moon-in'."

Moon Seizures

The belief in a connection between lunar activity and epilepsy is as old as the disease itself. A Latin Bible story that describes Jesus treating a child for epilepsy calls the ailment *lunaticus*, or "moonstruck." Greek mythology tells that Selene, goddess of the moon, punished those who had sinned against her by afflicting them with epileptic fits.

Early cures for epilepsy were linked to the moon. They included the plucking of peonies during certain phases of the moon and the use of powdered soapwort, at the time of the new moon, for three months. Silver, because of its pale color, was thought to have a special kinship with the moon and was prescribed in a variety of bizarre treatments, such as swallowing silver filings.

In the eighteenth century, Richard Mead, who had served as a British surgeon during several wars with France, claimed that new and full moons before battle brought on attacks of epilepsy among naval officers. "The power of the moon," he wrote, "was so greatly felt that it was not difficult to predict the occurrence of the attacks of the new or full moon."

In his *Manual of the Nervous Diseases of Man*, the nineteenth-century physician Dr. M. H. Romberg argued that ancient beliefs that the moon influenced epilepsy were quite correct. Because of his standing in the medical field, many other doctors took Romberg at his word.

In subsequent years, medical literature reported on the numbers of epileptic seizures said to occur during particular phases of the moon.

The willingness of medical researchers to link epilepsy to the moon continues. In his 1976 book, *Moon Madness*, E. L. Abel claims that a full moon increases overall electrical activity in the brain and "thus may be the basis for the periodicity in seizures experienced by those unfortunate people who suffer from the disease."

Did the Moon Make Them Do It?

No one knows exactly what dark forces of the mind lead people to take their own lives. Many researchers believe that the moon plays a role in suicides. While probably not the determining factor, the moon's influence—real or imagined—could be enough to give a final push to despairing individuals who decide to end their pain by killing themselves.

According to one of the earliest studies, conducted from 1964 to 1978 in Buffalo, New York, more suicides took place around a full moon than at any other time. A study of 928 suicides in Cayahoga County, Ohio, between 1972 and 1975, found that 120 people

145

Suicides are said to increase during certain phases of the moon.

took their lives on a new moon—a figure about 43 percent higher than at other times of the year.

The Golden Gate Bridge in San Francisco, a favorite spot for many who choose to end their lives by jumping into the waters below, has seen an increase of suicides during full moons.

Other studies have found that calls to suicide hotlines increase during different phases of the moon. For example, over a two-year period, the Suicide Prevention Center in Reno, Nevada, recorded more calls for help when the moon was new or at the first quarter than at other times.

In separate studies in Melbourne, Australia, and Winnipeg, Canada, researchers determined that women are more inclined to take their lives when the moon is at the first quarter.

Is the moon really an influence in suicide? It remains impossible to say because the studies are not consistent in identifying a common lunar phase.

Murder and Mayhem

There's no shortage of stories that can be told by police and fire fighters, ambulance drivers and paramedics, and emergency room doctors and nurses about the mayhem that breaks out when the moon is full.

Arson is said to increase, crimes against other individuals get particularly brutal and hospital admissions climb. It's even been noted that more fights break out during hockey games played on a full moon.

In a now classic study, psychologists Arnold Leiber and Carolyn Sherin reviewed 4,000 homicides that occurred between 1956 and 1970 in Miami and Cleveland. After completing the Miami study, Leiber wrote, "The results were astounding. Homicides in Dade County showed a striking correlation to the lunar phase cycle. Homicides peaked at the full moon." They peaked again, said Leiber, after a new moon. "Our results indicated that murders become more frequent with the increase in the moon's gravitational force."

After he turned his attention to Cleveland, Leiber noticed something odd. The peaks in homicides occurred about three days after both the full and new moon. He argued that his findings were still valid because they represented a "lag in the lunar effect" due to the different geographical locations.

The apparent lag between peaks of homicide activity in Miami and then Cleveland led Leiber to develop his controversial "biological tide" theory, published in *The Lunar Effect: Biolog-*

"But officer, the moon made me do it!"

ical Tides and Human Emotions (1978). Leiber said that hormonal activity in the brain is affected by the gravitational pull of the sun and the moon. Like the tides that occur at different times in different locations, so do people respond at different times to the effect of "biological tides." Leiber said "biological high tide sets the human machine on edge. These tides do not cause strange behavior. They only make it more likely to happen."

In subsequent years, other researchers have collected more evidence that ties violent human behavior to lunar phases. One of the most notorious murderers of the twentieth century, New York's "Son of Sam," killed five of his eight victims on nights when the moon was full or new.

Not surprisingly, many scientists have been extremely critical of theories, advanced by Leiber and others, that suggest that people are more likely to kill, set fires or commit other crimes when the moon is full.

Astronomer Nicholas Sanduleak tried to duplicate the Leiber findings in his own study of Cleveland homicides that took place over ten years beginning in 1971. He found no evidence of increases in murder around the time of the full or new moons. Also, in an at-

tempt to debunk the "biological tide" theory, Sanduleak found that the moon's greatest gravitational influence is when it is closest to earth. By contrast, when the moon is full or new it is actually farthest away from the earth.

In a blistering attack published in 1988 in *Psychological Bulletin*, physicist Roger Culver and psychologists James Rotton and I. W. Kelly charged that previous studies describing the "lunar effect on human behavior" were badly flawed. They argued that many of the studies were based on small sample sizes and short time periods and that they could not be replicated at a later date. They said that in light of the "lack of a reliable connection between lunar periods and human behavior and the generally negative results obtained in studies, it is suggested that the scientific community exercise great caution with regard to further studies claiming lunar effects on human behavior."

Dr. Melvin G. Goldzband, a spokesman for the San Diego Psychiatric Society, put it another way. Just before a full moon, he told the San Diego *Union* in 1985, "People don't realize how much trouble they invoke by their own expectations. When people take something like Friday the thirteenth or a full moon seriously, and they begin to dread what

Moon monster painted by a Crow Native American c. 1804. The Crow live predominantly in Montana, and parts of Wyoming and the Dakotas.

will happen on those days, trouble results. If you expect trouble to come, it'll come."

Terrors of the Night

The moon rules the night. Thus, creatures of the night, such as ghosts, demons, spirits, fairies, vampires, ghouls and the like, are the moon's children, thriving beneath her rays. The most fearsome of these creatures—and the ones most influenced by the moon— are the vampire and the werewolf.

The vampire has strong lunar associations through both eclipses and the werewolf of Slavic folklore. As was noted in "Moon Myths and Other Tales," one of the earliest meanings of "vampire" was an eclipse-eating dragon.

The term "vampire" came into the English language in the eighteenth century, when Austrian soldiers discovered the vampire cult in the remote villages of Austria-occupied Serbia. The soldiers were aghast at local beliefs that the dead returned to drain the blood and life of the living, and that to stop the attacks or prevent them, corpses which seemed to be uncorrupted were staked, cut into pieces, burned and severed of their heads. The specific be-

liefs about vampires, and the remedies against them, varied considerably from village to village.

149

The Serbian term from which "vampire" was borrowed is *vampir*, which in turn is equated with the Slavic terms *lampir, varcolaci, pricolici, vukodlak, vapir, vepir, upir, ala* and others, all of which have shades of meanings concerning different kinds of vampire-like creatures. Some are reanimated corpses, some are the spirits of the restless dead, some are creatures who can shapeshift to animals or humans, some are living humans who can shapeshift to animals—especially wolves. The term *vukodlak*, as well as a host of other equivalents of *vampir*, literally means

"wolf's hair." *Vampiri* were originally thought to transform themselves into wolves, as well as into dogs, cats, donkeys, horses and humans. According to one Eastern European superstition, when werewolves die they become vampires.

Bram Stoker drew on these superstitions when he wrote his classic thriller, *Dracula*, published in 1897. The protagonist, Count Dracula, is a reanimated corpse who lives on the blood of humans, and who has the power to shapeshift into bats and wolves, and to command animals and humans.

Peruvian vampire demon.

150

A witch turned into a werewolf attacks travelers. By Han Weiditz, 1517.

Howling at the Moon

The scene has been played out countless times in gothic novels and horror films: A man clutches his face and screams in agony. He falls to the ground and begins to thrash wildly as though racked in unimaginable pain. Animal fur springs forth from his hands, then his face, and finally covers him from head to toe. Soon he is no longer human, but transformed into a vicious, man-eating werewolf. He tears into the night, ready to maim and kill.

The one common ingredient in all these transformations is the full moon. From ancient to modern times, there have been many cases of people who suffer from delusions that they can turn into wolves when the moon is full. Medical science describes this condition as lycanthropy.

151

Why the full moon gets the credit or blame for triggering this seemingly demonic transformation—in cases real or imagined—is not known for sure. Perhaps it is an outgrowth of the image of the wolf howling at the moon.

Werewolf beliefs are universal and have existed since antiquity. In *Full Moons* (1981), a survey of the influence of the moon on human behavior, journalist Paul Katzeff writes that werewolves and lycanthropes "have crept into every culture past and present"—from the Navajo of the Southwestern United States who believed werewolves were nocturnal ghouls to Babylonian King Nebuchadnezzar who sunk so deeply into depression he finally imagined he had become a werewolf. Notes Katzeff, "Basically anyone could become a werewolf—all that's needed is a full moon . . . and perhaps an appropriate curse or potion."

According to most common legends, the werewolf is a person—usually a man but sometimes a woman—born under a curse that compels shapeshifting on nights of the full moon. Once changed, the werewolf roams about the countryside attacking and eating victims. In most tales, the werewolf is wounded, and the wound sympathetically carries over to the human form and thus reveals to others the true identity of the werewolf.

In other legends, the werewolf is a sorcerer or witch who deliberately transforms himself or herself in order to do evil. South American shamans and sorcerers are believed to turn themselves into werewolves—and other were-animals, such as weretigers—so that they can attack their enemies and drink their blood.

Ancient physicians of the classical world, such as Hippocrates (460-377 B.C.) and Galen (129-200 A.D.), believed that lycanthropy—called *Lycanthropia* by the Greeks and *Insania Lupina* by the Romans—was caused by an excess of melancholy. The human body was believed to be comprised of four basic humors corresponding to the four elements of earth, air, fire and water. Melancholy was associated with the earth and with bile. Excessive melancholy could cause mental derangement, including depression, hallucinations, delusions and insanity.

Werewolf beliefs were particularly strong in medieval times in Europe and the Baltic countries. During the Inquisition, werewolves, like witches, were said to operate under the devil's influence. The *Malleus Maleficarum* maintained that the shapeshifting was not real, but was an illusion created by the devil. The devil was said also to enter into the bodies of real wolves and cause them to go berserk.

During the Inquisition, various persons were tried as werewolves, along with accused witches, heretics and other enemies of the Church. Their "confessions" are suspect, since they usually followed severe and barbaric torture. In 1573 in Dole, France, Gilles Garnier was tried as a werewolf and was convicted for the murder of several children. He confessed that he killed a

ten-year-old girl with his teeth and claws, stripped off her clothes and ate part of her. He took the rest of her flesh home to his wife. He also confessed to strangling a ten-year-old boy, biting off his leg and eating his thighs and belly. Garnier was attacking another victim when several peasants recognized his face despite his wolf's form, as they solemnly testified. Garnier was burned alive.

One of the most famous and lurid werewolf trials was the 1589 case of Peter Stubb (also called Stube or Stumpf) of Bedburg near Cologne. After being tortured on the rack, Stubb confessed to practicing the "wicked arts" from the age of twelve years. He said the devil had given him a magic belt that enabled him to change into, according to the trial records, "the likenes of a greedy deuouring Woolf, strong and mighty, with eyes great and large, which in the night sparkeled like vnto brandes of fire, a mouth great and wide, with most sharpe and cruell teeth, A huge body, and mightye pawes." Stubb could return to his human shape by removing the belt.

Stubb described himself as an "insatiable bloodsucker" who fed happily on children, women, men, lambs, sheep and goats. He even confessed to killing his own son and eating his brains, as well as to murdering and eating thirteen other children and two pregnant women, feasting on their fetuses. His murder sprees were accompanied by an insatiable lust, Stubb confessed, and he said he fornicated with his daughter, assorted mistresses and a succubus sent to him by the devil.

What makes Stubb's case particularly astonishing is that he allegedly committed these atrocities for twenty-five years before being exposed. No one noticed? Probably Stubb merely fell afoul of the authorities, and someone decided he was a werewolf. According to the records, he was captured when hunters ran him down in his wolf form, and he took off his belt and was recognized.

Werewolf cases continue into modern times, involving individuals who genuinely believe they transform themselves into wolves. Such cases are rare in industrialized countries, but occur more frequently in China, India, Africa and Central and South America, perhaps because higher proportions of the population in those countries live closer to myth and superstition. Delusions involve not only wolves, but leopards, elephants, crocodiles, sharks, buffalo, tigers, jaguars, eagles, serpents and other feared animals. Modern lycanthropes exhibit the primary symptoms described since ancient times: an altered state of consciousness; the posture, voice and other attributes of the animal on which they are fixed; alienation from self and society; bestial compulsions, such as desire to consume raw flesh; acute physiological stress and anxiety; and obsession with the demonic. Unlike earlier lycanthropes, most twentieth-century lycanthropes do not engage in murder, cannibalism or sexual violence. Some may kill and eat small animals, while others take to howling at the moon and sleeping in graveyards.

One modern case of lycanthropy was the story of a "Mr. W.," as reported in 1975 in the *Canadian Psychiatric Association Journal*. The subject was a thirty-seven-year-old Appalachian farmer. Shortly after his discharge from the U.S. Navy, Mr. W. began to show little interest in his farm chores or other daily activities. He let his facial hair grow, making believe that it was fur. More than once he was found sleeping in cemeteries, and occasionally he would lie down on highways in front of approaching traffic. He howled at the moon. Mr. W. said he had become a werewolf.

He was admitted to a psychiatric hospital, where doctors found that he was suffering from a chronic brain syndrome of undetermined origin, resulting in chronic undifferentiated schizophrenia. But doctors also concluded that the occurrence of his psychosis during the full moon remained unexplained on an organic level.

It is likely that drug-induced psychosis accounts for a portion of lycanthropy cases old and modern. Hallucinogens such as jimsonweed, peyote, henbane, nightshade, opium and LSD produce altered states of consciousness in which there are perceptual distortions and a loss of ego boundaries.

One such case was that of "Mr. H.," a twenty-year-old man from Appalachia who was studied by doctors in the 1970s. While in Europe with the U. S. Army, Mr. H. ingested LSD in the woods and felt himself transform into a werewolf. He could see and feel fur grow on his hands and face. He experienced a sudden and overwhelming desire to chase rabbits and devour them live. He also felt he could look into what he called "the devil's world."

Mr. H. wandered in the woods for two days in this terrible state, and then returned to the army when he felt that his appearance was normal. However, he remained convinced that he was still a werewolf. And when he noticed that the mess hall put up a sign saying "feeding time," he was convinced that others were aware of his secret.

A psychiatric examination revealed that Mr. H. had a long history of taking hallucinogens, and suffered from paranoid delusions, delusions of grandeur and acute schizophrenia. After treatment with medication, he quit believing that he was a werewolf, but remained preoccupied with satanism and was haunted by the feeling that the devil could insert thoughts in his mind.

Fairy Power

Fairy rings are circles of inedible mushrooms that grow naturally in grassy places in Europe, Britain and North America. They often spring up after a rain. According to lore, they provide convenient magical circles where fairies and witches meet, dance and sing at night. In Britain the rings are also called *hag tracks* because, according to lore, they are created by the dancing feet of witches.

Superstition holds that if a person stands in a fairy ring under a full moon and makes a wish, the wish will come true. Another superstition says that to see fairies, who are usually invisible except to those with second sight, one must run around a fairy ring nine times under a full moon. But don't do it on May Eve or All Hallow's Eve, the two major fairy festivals, because the fairies will be offended and carry you off to Elfland.

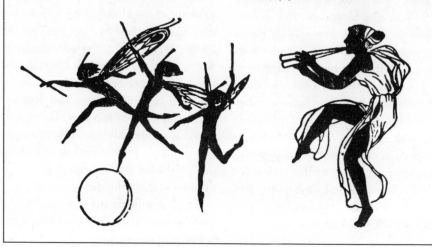

According to folklore, moonlight brings the fairies out to dance and play in their secret groves.

Visiting Count Dracula

When Bram Stoker wrote his classic thriller, *Dracula* (1897), about a vampire who travels from Transylvania to England to terrorize residents of London, he made ample use of the moon as a backdrop to chilling action. Stoker's artful use of moonlit scenes set a standard for vampire stories in both fiction and film: the moon is full, somewhere a wolf howls, and the vampire stalks its prey.

Dracula begins with the journey of British legal clerk Jonathan Harker to Transylvania to arrange for Count Dracula (of whom he knows nothing) to purchase an estate in London. He travels by coach at night through the Carpathian Mountains to Dracula's castle. Along the way, Harker is frightened by natives who warn him not to travel at night. At the Borgo Pass, he transfers to a coach sent by the count. Harker describes in his diary the harrowing, moonlit final leg of the journey.

"At last there came a time when the driver went further afield than he had yet gone, and during his absence the horses began to tremble worse than ever and to snort and scream with fright. I could not see any cause for it, for the howling of the wolves had ceased altogether; but just then the moon, sailing through the black clouds, appeared behind the jagged crest of a beetling, pine-clad rock, and by its light I saw around us a ring of wolves, with white teeth and lolling red tongues, with long sinewy limbs and shaggy hair. They were a hundred times more terrible in the grim silence which held them than even when they howled. For myself, I felt a sort of paralysis of fear. It is only when a man feels himself face to face with such horrors that he can understand their true import.

"All at once the wolves began to howl as though the moonlight had had some peculiar effect on them. The horses jumped around and reared, and looked helplessly round with eyes that rolled in a painful way to see; but the living ring of terror encompassed them on every side, and they had perforce to remain within it. I called to the coachman to come, for it seemed to me that our only chance was to try to break out through the ring, and to aid his approach I shouted and beat the side of the caléche, hoping by the noise to scare the wolves from that side, so as to give him a chance of reaching the trap. How he came there, I know not, but I heard his voice raised in a tone of imperious command, and looking towards the sound, saw him stand in the roadway. As he swept his long arms, as though brushing aside some impalpable obstacle, the wolves fell back and back further still. Just then a heavy cloud passed across the face of the moon, so that we were again in darkness.

"When I could see again the driver was climbing into the caléche, and the wolves had disappeared. This was all so strange and uncanny that a dreadful fear came upon me, and I was afraid to speak or move. The time seemed interminable as we swept on our way, now in almost complete darkness, for the rolling clouds obscured the moon. We kept on ascending, with occasional periods of quick descent, but in the main always ascending. Suddenly I became conscious of the fact that the driver was in the act of pulling up the horses in the courtyard of a vast ruined castle, from whose tall black windows came no ray of light, and whose broken battlements allowed a jagged line against the moonlit sky."

At the castle, Harker meets the mysterious and ugly count. It isn't long before the young clerk realizes he has become a prisoner of the castle. Strange things happen at night beneath the baleful rays of the moon. One night, Harker looks out from the window of his room and, to his horror, spies the count

emerge from a window below and creep like a lizard down the wall of the castle. "I thought it was some trick of the moonlight, some weird effect of shadow; but I kept looking and it could be no delusion," Harker writes in his diary.

The next night, Harker awakens to see brilliant moonlight streaming into his room. Framed in the light are three beautiful young women. He notices that though the moon is behind them, they cast no shadows on the floor. They have voluptuous red lips and their white teeth shine in the moonlight. The women are the count's vampire consorts, and they have come to drink

Harker's blood. But before they can do so, the count enters and forbids them to touch Harker.

As Harker's nightmare imprisonment continues he learns more about the count and the vampire women. He realizes that at some point the count will kill him, and his nights are filled with terror. One night Harker sits by his window, and suddenly notices little specks floating in the rays of the moonlight. They seem to be dust, and they whirl and collect in small shapes around him. In the valley below the castle, dogs begin to howl, and the howling seems to make the specks dance faster and take new shapes in the moonbeams, hypnotizing him with their movements.

"Quicker and quicker danced the dust, and the moonbeams seemed to quiver as they went by me into the mass of gloom beyond," Harker writes. "More and more they gathered until they seemed to take dim phantom shapes. And then I started, broad awake and in full possession of my senses, and ran screaming from the place. The phantom shapes, which were becoming gradually materialized from the moonbeams, were those of the three ghostly women to whom I was doomed. I fled, and felt somewhat safer in my room, where there was no moonlight and where the lamp was burning brightly."

Harker escapes and the count and his women travel to England. Time and again, Stoker uses the moon to create a half-lit world where fears take physical shape and the unthinkable becomes real. Mina Murray, Harker's fiancee and then bride, sees moonlight frame a great bat wheeling across the sky. The moon shines high in the sky the night the wolf Bersicker (Berserker) goes howling mad in the zoological gardens and escapes. Moonlight graces the sleeping faces of the count's victims and lights the cemetery where Lucy Westenra, victim-turned-vampire, stalks her own prey.

When the count meets his grisly end by being stabbed through the heart, the action takes place in the daytime, for only in the sun's domain is the vampire powerless against his hunters.

Man on the Moon and Beyond

United States Postal Service stamps issued in 1989 commemorating the twentieth anniversary of Apollo 11 moon landing.

For millennia, human beings have traveled to the moon and explored its mysteries in their imagination and fantasies. As early as 165 A.D., Lucian of Samos conceived a fictional voyage to the moon, where the explorers found an enormous mirror suspended over a shallow well. The mirror enabled them to see every city and nation on earth as clearly as if they were standing directly overhead. It was only a matter of time before technology enabled the voyage of the moon to be taken in reality. The modern explorers found no mirror, but they did look at earth and saw it clearly as a unified whole, the home of humanity.

Dreaming of Man on the Moon

When the crew of Apollo 11 set their lunar landing craft down on the moon in July 1969, they did more than make history. They validated the dreams of countless men and women who had labored long and hard for that day, often against a background of frustration and dashed hopes.

This first manned moon landing followed a short but dramatic history of unmanned missions that had tested the patience of just about everyone involved. It was a period marked by numerous U.S. and Soviet failures, repeated cost overruns, government inquiries, as well as delay and growing public disappointment. Yet, sandwiched between the failures, there were successes. And with each successful mission, America came closer to answering the challenge, made by President John F. Kennedy in his 1961 State of the Union address, to land a man on the moon and return him safely to earth "before this decade is over."

Looking back, that ten-year window which the president opened for his countrymen was a very narrow one.

161

While scientists had been experimenting with rocket propulsion since World War II, the race to the moon did not begin in earnest until the night of October 4, 1957, when the Soviets rocked the world with their startling announcement that they had put into orbit the first artificial satellite, a twenty-eight-pound (12.7 kilogram) object named Sputnik.

America responded three months later, successfully launching Explorer 1 on January 30, 1958. However, as scientists soon discovered, sending a satellite into space and reaching the moon by rocket were entirely different challenges. Nonetheless, buoyed by the success of Explorer 1, America launched Pioneer 1 toward the moon on October 11, 1958. The first attempt to hit the moon was a dismal failure—the spacecraft missed its target by 71,000 miles (114,239 kilometers). Pioneer 2 (November 8, 1958) fizzled as well, and Pioneer 3 did little better than Pioneer 1.

In their efforts to reach the moon with unmanned crafts, the Soviets seemed to have better luck. Although Luna 1 (January 1, 1959) only came within 4,600 miles (7401 kilometers) of the surface, the moon suddenly appeared within reach. Proof of that came

nine months later in September when Luna 2 became the first spacecraft from earth to crash-land on the moon. The following month, the USSR sent Luna 3 around the moon, and the world saw the first photographs of the far side.

The next American chapter in the story of space exploration came with the advent of the Ranger program, which began in 1960. According to statements by the National Aeronautics and Space Administration (NASA) officials, Ranger was designed to provide by photographs information about the nature of the lunar surface that astronomers would not be able to detect by "peering through the thick layer of atmosphere around the earth." Photos of the lunar surface would help scientists prepare for manned landings.

Unfortunately, the Ranger program had anything but an auspicious beginning. While the first two Ranger missions were test flights, Ranger 3, launched on January 26, 1962, was targeted to reach the moon. It missed by 22,000 miles (35,398 kilometers). The following April, Ranger 4 crashed into the far side of the moon because of problems with its control system. Ranger 5 (October 19, 1962) missed the moon completely, bringing a congressional inquiry in its wake.

Soviet space flight stamp issued in 1969.

Delayed for a year, but seemingly back on track, the Ranger program resumed with the launch of number six on January 30, 1964. With all systems functioning and the craft on course, America appeared to be on the verge of its first major success. Author Richard S. Lewis, in *Appointment on the Moon* (1969), captured the mood at mission control headquarters inside the Jet Propulsion Laboratory at the California Institute of Technology shortly after 3 A.M., Sunday, February 2, as Ranger 6 neared the moon: "Now that the moment of triumph was near, all of the disappointments and frustrations of the past seemed to be erased. Scientists, engineers, technicians and secretaries and clerks waited silently for the announcement that the pictures were coming—the first close-up pictures of the moon. But no picture signals came. Ranger 6 smashed into the moon. Even though Ranger 6 had been checked and rechecked . . . it too failed, and it appeared that the Ranger mission was beyond the capability of the space program."

The sense of doom disappeared quickly. Six months later, on July 31, 1964, Ranger 7 sent back 4,000 high quality photos for astronomers to study. Ranger brought the surface of the moon

within a viewing distance of one-half mile (804 meters). By comparison, astronomers on earth, could magnify the moon to an apparent distance of 500 miles (806 kilometers).

Thankfully, the three subsequent Ranger missions were as fruitful, producing over 17,225 photographs.

Meanwhile, the Ranger missions stirred up a new debate over a theory that had been introduced in 1955 by Dr. Thomas Gold, an astronomer who was then with the Royal Greenwich Observatory in England. Gold claimed that the surface of the moon was comprised of soft dust and that upon landing a spacecraft and all its gear would sink into oblivion.

Although this theory did not have universal support from either U.S. or Soviet scientists, the only way to disprove it was to send a spacecraft to the moon, land it gently and see what happened.

That task fell to the Soviets. Following a string of failed attempts, Luna 9 successfully made a soft touchdown near Oceanus Procellarum. Astronomer Patrick Moore, writing in *Guide to the Moon* (1976), noted that "Luna 9 was standing on a hard layer, with no tendency to sink, so that Gold's dust theory was completely wrong. Potential

Soviet stamps commemorating twentieth anniversary of 1969 American manned moon landing.

astronauts felt comforted. If a manned craft were to land, the moon would at least refrain from swallowing it up."

America followed with the Surveyor program, launching seven missions between May 1966 and January 1968. From the five successful soft landings, American scientists concurred with what the Russians had discovered earlier.

Following Surveyor 1, Robert J. Parks, a project manager, said, "I think you can state that in this particular area where Surveyor landed, the way it landed, you certainly would expect the lunar module to be able to land."

In addition to testing the firmness of the lunar surface, several of the Surveyor missions carried out a variety of analyses of moon soil, including measurements of its chemical composition. One of the findings was that the lunar surface was composed of basalt much like that found on earth.

Surveyor marked the last of the American unmanned launches to the moon. Other unmanned missions, such as the five Orbiter spacecraft launched by America between August 1966 and August 1967, were designed to photograph all of the moon's surface. Manned spaceflights, meanwhile, were limited to orbits around the earth.

The Apollo Program

The Apollo program to send astronauts to the moon was announced in May 1961, long before decisions were made on technology and methods that would accomplish the job. While research was conducted, the path to the moon was paved by two manned space programs, Mercury and Gemini. On May 5, 1961, America put its first man in space. He was Alan B. Shepard, Jr., whose flight in the tiny, one-person Mercury Freedom 7 was a suborbital arc that lasted fifteen minutes and landed in the ocean 302 miles (486 kilometers) downrange from Cape Canaveral (since renamed Cape Kennedy), Florida. Shepard was not the first man in space, however; the Russians had succeeded in orbiting cosmonaut Yuri A. Gargarin on April 12, 1961. Russia put in orbit a second man, Gherman S. Titov, before America succeeded with its first manned orbital flight by John Glenn, Jr., in the Friendship 7 on February 20, 1962. It appeared as though the Soviet Union might beat America to the moon, and the race was on. To reach the moon by the end of the 1960s required a tremendous jump in rocket technology, pushing the state of the art to new limits. NASA rose to the challenge.

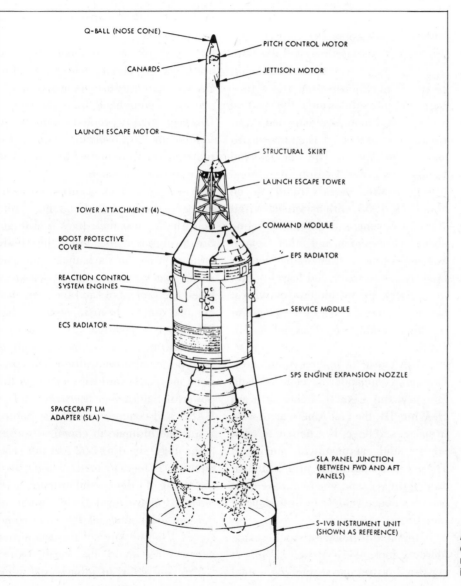

Q-BALL (NOSE CONE)

PITCH CONTROL MOTOR

CANARDS

JETTISON MOTOR

LAUNCH ESCAPE MOTOR

STRUCTURAL SKIRT

LAUNCH ESCAPE TOWER

TOWER ATTACHMENT (4)

COMMAND MODULE

BOOST PROTECTIVE
COVER

EPS RADIATOR

REACTION CONTROL
SYSTEM ENGINES

SERVICE MODULE

ECS RADIATOR

SPS ENGINE EXPANSION NOZZLE

SPACECRAFT LM
ADAPTER (SLA)

SLA PANEL JUNCTION
(BETWEEN FWD AND AFT
PANELS)

S-IVB INSTRUMENT UNIT
(SHOWN AS REFERENCE)

Apollo spacecraft consisted of command, service and lunar modules. Lunar module is drawn in dotted lines.

165

The Mercury program ended in 1963 with Gordon Cooper's thirty-four-hour orbit around the earth aboard the Faith 7. NASA then advanced to the Gemini program, in which two men at a time were sent into orbit around the earth in a bigger and more sophisticated craft. Gemini was conceived as an intermediate step to Apollo. The first manned Gemini craft was Gemini 3, dubbed "Molly Brown," which lifted off on March 23, 1965, with astronauts Virgil "Gus" Grissom and John W. Young aboard. These men and other Gemini astronauts practiced changing their orbital planes in space and learning how to perform extravehicular activities. Gemini 12 was the last in the program, its flight ending on November 12, 1966.

NASA chose for its first Apollo crew Grissom, commander, a veteran of both Mercury and Gemini flights; Edward H. White III, the first American to walk in space; and Roger B. Chaffee, a Naval officer and aeronautical engineer. These three would ride in a craft that was bigger yet, and was by far the most complex space vehicle built to date by the U.S.

In terms of technology, Apollo made Mercury look like a Model T Ford. It consisted of two parts weighing a total of 45 tons (40.8 metric tons): a command module, which would serve as the cockpit and living quarters of the crew, and a service module, with a powerful, 21,500-pound-thrust engine that would drive the ship back from the moon. However, quality problems, equipment failures and cost overruns in the ambitious program threatened to jeopardize the quest for the moon.

A serious setback occurred on January 27, 1967, when Grissom, White and Chaffee lost their lives in a tragic fire during a rehearsal test of the Apollo craft as it sat on its launch pad. The sealed cockpit became a deathtrap when fire broke out, and the men succumbed quickly to toxic gases, probably carbon monoxide.

Following an investigation and a brief period of turmoil, the Apollo program moved forward with testing of the powerful Saturn 5 booster rocket that NASA had commissioned. The Saturn 5 was the ultimate in chemical rocket technology, standing 362 feet tall (110 meters), 62 feet (19 meters) taller than the Statue of Liberty, and weighing 310 tons (281 metric tons). It was capable of 8.7 million pounds of thrust in three stages. No one knew if this giant and heavy bird would fly. Furthermore, NASA was able to afford only nine rockets instead of the fifteen originally planned, which meant fewer tests if NASA was going to meet the end-of-the-decade goal.

Fly the Saturn 5 did, spectacularly though not reliably. Unmanned Apollo craft were launched in tests between November 9, 1967, and April 4, 1968. Despite initial successes, problems with vibrations developed due to variations in engine thrust. Engineers called it the "pogo effect." Apollo 5 was a dismal failure when the descent engine shut down prematurely. Apollo 6 suffered a third-stage failure.

Engineers set to work to correct the pogo effect and other problems. Due to finances, a decision was made to forgo another unmanned test, and NASA proceeded directly to the first manned test with Apollo 7. The crew, Walter Cunningham, Donn F. Eisele and Walter M. Shirra, Jr., commander, lifted off on October 11, 1968, for orbits around the earth. The flight went smoothly, despite the fact that the crew contracted colds. They completed 163 orbits around the earth. All systems were go for the first manned shot to the moon.

Apollo 8 was launched December 21, 1968, with William A. Anders, Frank Borman, commander, and James A. Lovell, Jr., aboard. Their goal was

Giant Saturn V rocket boosters launched Apollo missions into space.

to orbit around the moon, reaching a perilune (closest point) of a mere 69 miles (111 kilometers), then head back to earth to land in the Indian Ocean. The mission was a brilliant success.

Five potential sites were identified for the first manned moon landing by American astronauts. Apollo 8's mission was to sight, track and photograph at least one site. The Sea of Tranquility, site number one, was chosen.

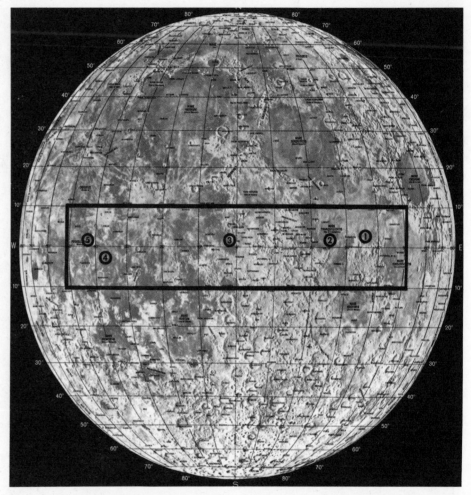

It took the craft 66 hours to reach the moon. Early in the trip, the crew reported illness that they ascribed to a form of motion sickness due to their weightlessness. Borman was hit the worst. They apparently recovered quickly.

As their craft swung into orbit around the moon, the first human beings to view the lunar surface close-up were awed by what they saw. Their descriptions were augmented by television pictures they transmitted back to an equally awed international audience on earth.

"What does the ole moon look like from sixty [nautical] miles?" inquired Major Gerald P. Carr (U.S. Marine Corps) from Mission Control in Houston.

Responded Lovell, "The moon is essentially gray, no color. Looks like plaster of Paris or sort of a deep grayish sand."

The crew were able to identify numerous surface features on both the near and far sides, from maps they had studied earlier. On December 24, after several orbits, the crew shared their impressions and feelings about the moon. Borman found it "a vast, lonely, forbidding type of existence, a great expanse of nothing, that looks rather like clouds and clouds of pumice stone, and it certainly would not be a very inviting place to live or work."

Lovell agreed, adding that he found the vast loneliness awe-inspiring, "and it makes you realize just what you have back there on earth." Anders said he was impressed by the starkness of the terrain, and the beautiful lunar sunrises and sunsets.

The crew turned their cameras on earth to show what the home planet looked like from the moon. For the first time in history, human beings saw their home from a point in space a quarter of a million miles away. It was a round, cloud-swathed pearl, far more awe-inspiring and moving than the moon viewed from the earth. It was an exquisite moment that expanded the consciousness of humanity forever.

Aware of the significance of that sight, the Apollo 8 crew sent a message to fellow earthlings: they took turns

The Apollo 8 crew were awed by the sight of the earth rising above the moon.

reading Genesis 1:1-10, the story of the creation of the universe.

Apollo 8 was a smashing success, yet the key piece of the lunar program remained untested: the lunar module, a third piece of Apollo that would separate from the command module while in orbit around the moon and take two men on the perilous trip to the moon's surface and back to the command module. The lunar module was tested in orbit around the earth by Apollo 9 (March 3, 1969), whose crew comprised James McDivitt, commander, David R. Scott and Russell L. "Rusty" Schweickart. The lunar module was given its second and last test by Apollo 10 (May 18, 1969). Crew members Eugene A. Cernan, Thomas P. Stafford, commander, and John W. Young flew to the moon, where the command module entered into orbit. Stafford and Cernan, in the lunar module, descended to 50,000 feet (15.24 kilometers) above the moon's surface. They were to fly over one of the designated landing points for Apollo, Landing Point No. 2 in the Mare Tranquillitatus, but due to a navigational error, missed it by 5 or 6 miles (about 8.8 kilometers). They returned successfully to the command module. The next step was to send a crew directly to the lunar soil.

The Eagle Lands

The honor of being the first humans on the moon fell to the crew of Apollo 11. Neil A. Armstrong, 38, a civilian, commanded the crew. Armstrong had been a combat pilot for the Navy during the Korean War. The other crew members were Colonel Edwin E. "Buzz" Aldrin, Jr., 39, and Air Force Lieutenant Colonel Michael Collins, 38.

Apollo 11 lifted off on schedule on July 16, 1969. The flight to the moon was smooth and uneventful, and the command module, named Columbia, settled into lunar orbit. On Sunday, July 20, Armstrong and Aldrin entered the lunar module, named Eagle, and began their descent. Collins remained behind in the command module. The entire world held its breath—even Pope Paul VI arranged for a color television to be installed at his summer residence so that he could watch the flight.

The Eagle overshot the landing site by about four miles, still landing in the Mare Tranquillitatus, but near a rocky area called Cat's Paw. At 4:17 P.M. plus 42 seconds Eastern Daylight Savings Time, Armstrong announced, "Houston, Tranquillity Base here. The Eagle has landed." The world cheered.

After several hours rest, Armstrong

Apollo 11 astronaut Edwin E. "Buzz" Aldrin stands beside the first US flag raised on lunar soil. The photograph was taken by Neil Armstrong, mission commander. Astronauts' footprints are visible in foreground.

Apollo 11 astronauts found a thin layer of powder on the moon's surface. Their footprints will remain indefinitely.

onto the moon. It was an eerie sight: the stark, alien landscape, the harsh lights and shadows, and a man in a bulky spacesuit floating down through the air with the grace of a ballet dancer.

Armstrong set his foot down into a fine gray powder less than an inch (2.5 centimeters) in thickness. It seemed to have the consistency of powdered charcoal and adhered to his boots. His footprints were sharp and clear in it.

The first task Armstrong performed was the taking of still photographs with a camera. Then he took a long-handled scoop and quickly collected about two pounds (907 grams) of rocks and soil from the immediate vicinity. These were stored in a leg pouch. Thus, if an emergency arose and the Eagle had to depart prematurely, the crew would return to earth with at least a sample of lunar material.

Armstrong then set up a solar wind experiment. He unrolled a sheet of aluminum foil that captured the solar wind, a stream of particles that shoots out from the sun through space.

It was now time for Aldrin to emerge from the Eagle and join Armstrong on the surface. The men found walking in the low gravity easier than anticipated. For the television camera that was transmitting the historic occasion live

and Aldrin were given permission to leave the Eagle and set foot on the moon. They followed a carefully planned program. They would have only two-and-a-half hours on the surface, during which they had to collect rock and soil samples and set up scientific experiments.

As Armstrong began to climb down the ladder, he deployed a television camera that would record his first step

Say It Again, Neil

Anyone who was watching television or listening to the radio on July 20, 1969, will never forget the words of Neil A. Armstrong when he took his first step onto the moon. With the whole world watching and listening, he uttered the oft-repeated line: "That's one small step for man, one giant leap for mankind."

Unfortunately, that's not what he meant to say.

Armstrong should have said, "That's one small step for a man, one giant leap for mankind." By forgetting to say the "a," he said he was taking both a small step and a giant leap for all of mankind.

Initially, NASA attempted to say that the "a" had been uttered but lost in radio transmission. Armstrong later admitted that, in the excitement, he probably just forgot to say it.

back to earth, they demonstrated a kangaroo hop that looked like weird acrobatics.

To commemorate the occasion, they planted an American flag in the soil (as would all subsequent Apollo missions that reached the moon). Earlier, there had been discussion of planting a United Nations flag, but Congress, swelled with national pride at being the first nation to the moon, insisted on the Stars and Stripes. President Richard M. Nixon, speaking by telephone from the Oval Office at the White House and patched through by Mission Control, congratulated the astronauts. "I just can't tell you how proud we all are of what you have done," the president said. "Because of what you have done, the heavens have become a part of man's world. And as you talk to us from the Sea of Tranquility it inspires us to

"Buzz" Aldrin poses in the Sea of Tranquility.

Apollo 11 commander Neil A. Armstrong, the first human being on the moon.

double our efforts to bring peace and tranquility to earth. For one priceless moment, in the whole history of man, all the people on this earth are truly one."

Armstrong and Aldrin then commenced the rest of their scheduled extravehicular activity (EVA). They collected some thirty pounds (13.6 kilograms) of rocks and soil, selecting various kinds as had been previously identified by spacecraft photographs. They found the surface puzzling. Underneath the loose powder were surprisingly hard soil and rock that were difficult to penetrate by digging straight down. Yet, if they dug sideways, the material gave like muck or wet sand.

The men also set up seismometer and laser reflector experiments. Because of the low gravity, they worked more slowly than anticipated. They had to hurry to collect an additional twenty pounds (9 kilograms) of rocks. After two hours and twenty-five minutes, with their oxygen and water running low, they were ordered to return to the Eagle and depart.

The next day, Monday, July 21, was declared a national holiday in the U.S. Other countries celebrated as well. Apollo 11 returned to earth on July 22. The crew was whisked off to a 21-day

quarantine at the Lunar Receiving Laboratory, a special, eight-million-dollar, 87,000-square-foot (808-square-kilometer) facility near the Manned Space Center in Houston. There they were debriefed, subjected to various biological tests and allowed to relax.

The rocks and soil samples, stored carefully in vacuum containers, were also delivered to the Lunar Receiving Laboratory. There had been a great deal of concern about the potential hazard of contamination by unknown microbes, should any be found to exist on the moon. The probability was extremely low; nonetheless, stringent quarantine and antiseptic conditions were established so that nothing from the moon could escape the facility. Even the air inside the Lunar Receiving Laboratory was sterilized and then exhausted outside.

Roughly five percent of the fifty pounds (22.6 kilograms) of samples were subjected to biological tests, consisting of exposure to different culture media and to a variety of earth life forms, including germ-free mice, Japanese quail (which have a rapid reproductive cycle), shellfish, cockroaches and numerous plants. The remaining forty percent were subjected to optical, mineralogic, petrographic, chemical, magnetic, radiation, X-ray diffraction and fluorescence tests. After a fifty- to eighty-day quarantine and test period, a few pounds of samples were distributed to scientists throughout the U.S. and several other nations.

Undoubtedly, some scientists hoped to find living organisms, thus answering the question, "Are we alone in the universe?" However, the samples revealed the moon to be a sterile world.

Even in the flush of Apollo 11's success, the U.S. manned space program was beginning to end. National economic problems had already forced cuts in NASA's budget, and layoffs began after employment in the program peaked in 1967. Following Apollo 11, the program called for an additional nine manned flights to the moon, ending with Apollo 20 in 1972.

It was not to be. The program did end in 1972, but with Apollo 17. Apollos 12 through 17 were each sent to different locations on the moon and had different objectives. Each faced new dangers.

Apollo 12 followed Apollo 11 by four months, still in the afterglow of Apollo 11's fame. The Apollo 12 crew, Charles "Pete" Conrad, Jr., commander, Alan L. Bean and Richard F. "Dick" Gordon, Jr., had the unenviable role of being second on the moon. As Conrad observed, "Nobody ever remembers what the second person to do something does." Nonetheless, the Apollo 12 crew were the first to have fun on the moon. Conrad in particular was noted for his jokes and giddy laughter during the EVA.

Apollo 12 blasted off on November 12, 1969. Seconds after clearing the launch pad, the Saturn 5 booster was struck by lightning and lost its primary electrical systems. Quick thinking by Bean activated the backup systems, averting disaster. The craft—the command module Columbia and the lunar module Intrepid—continued on to the moon.

One of Apollo 12's assignments was to retrieve a piece of Surveyor III, which had soft-landed in the rolling crater field of Oceanus Procellarum (Ocean of Storms) in April 1967. This required a pinpoint landing. There would be no room to overshoot like Apollo 11 had done.

Conrad and Bean brought the lunar module down within walking distance of the Surveyor, which rested at the bottom of Snowman crater. Their itinerary called for them to spend 32 hours on the moon, 10 hours longer than Apollo 11. During that time, they took two moon walks, one for 4 hours and 1 minute and the other for 3 hours and 32 minutes. Their second walk extended a total of 6000 feet (1.8 kilometers). The Apollo 11 moonwalk had extended only about 200 feet (61 meters) from the lunar module. Conrad and Bean collected rock and soil samples, retrieved the piece of Surveyor III and activated a portable nuclear power plant that NASA officials hoped would run scientific equipment (called ALSEP, for Apollo Lunar Scientific Experiments Package) for a year. (The devices left behind by Apollo 11 had run out of electricity after a few days.) The only thing that malfunctioned was a television camera that was supposed to transmit the first live color pictures of moonwalks. At one point, Bean nearly stumbled and fell backwards into Snowman crater, which probably would have been fatal. He was saved by a warning shout from Conrad.

Apollo 13 bore out superstitions about the bad luck associated with the number thirteen. The mission, with James A. Lovell, Jr., commander, John L. "Jack" Swigert and Fred W. Haise, Jr., was to land in Fra Mauro, an area of deep canyons and valleys and high mountains, and determine definitely whether the moon was geologically alive or dead—that is, whether or not it contained or had ever contained a molten core like the earth's.

Liftoff took place on April 11, 1970. But on the night of April 13, when the craft was 200,000 miles (321,800 kilometers) out from earth, an oxygen tank exploded. A second explosion in another oxygen tank knocked out two of the craft's three main fuel cells, which meant the craft could not land on the moon. The one remaining fuel cell was sufficient to return the craft to earth—if the oxygen supply lasted. The mission was aborted, but in order to return to earth, the craft had to continue on to the moon, swing around it and get a slingshot effect back. With oxygen spewing out into space, Apollo 13 hurtled on with the lives of the crew hanging in balance.

The swing around the moon was completed successfully, but then the crew faced other life-threatening hazards. A battery vented gas, threatening to explode. It didn't. In order to conserve power, the backup electrical system was powered down, bringing the heat in the mother ship to a low of 38 degrees Fahrenheit (3 degrees Celsius), and causing a dangerously high level of carbon dioxide in the air. In addition, inadequate water limited each crewman to drinking only two ounces a day.

Against the odds, Apollo 13 returned safely to earth on April 17. NASA delayed the next lunar mission until engineering changes were made to prevent another similar accident.

Meanwhile, public interest in the moon missions had dropped tremendously. Even the cliffhanger of Apollo 13 could not generate much interest in the forthcoming Apollo 14. NASA, under financial attack, had to justify the $400 million price tag for Apollo 14.

The program, though troubled, continued. Apollo 14, with the lunar module Antares, was launched on January 31, 1971 with Alan B. Shepard, Jr., commander, Edgar D. Mitchell and Stuart A. Roosa aboard.

The Antares set down in Fra Mauro on February 5. The following day Shepard and Mitchell set out for Cone Crater, the selected site for their experiments. They took a Modular Equipment Transporter, dubbed the "golf cart," filled with equipment. They became lost, however, deceived by the slopes and by the angle of the sun. They were forced to give up on Cone Crater, but they did collect 93 pounds (42 kilograms) of rocks, some of the oldest gathered to date. Shepard also made history as the first extraterrestrial golfer, hitting golf balls with a six-iron.

The Apollo 14 men were the last moon-walkers. The next crews would drive around the moon in Lunar Rovers, buggies with four-wheel drive.

Mitchell's Psychic Tests

During his rest periods on Apollo 14's flight to the moon, astronaut Edgar D. Mitchell conducted secret and unofficial tests for extrasensory perception (ESP). Mitchell was intensely interested in parapsychology and "noesis," a philosophical term pertaining to the highest knowledge.

Mitchell had arranged with four persons on earth a telepathy experiment. He was curious to see if being in outer space would have a noticeable influence upon results. During his rests, he concentrated on sequences of numbers, holding the images in his mind. He worked with sets of twenty-five random numbers each.

He completed two hundred number sequences. A mean chance score of correct guesses was forty. After the mission was over, Mitchell reported that two of his four subjects had correctly guessed fifty-one sequences, "far exceeding anything expected," he said, but still only "moderately significant."

Mitchell left the NASA program after Apollo 14 and retired from the Navy in October 1972. In March 1973, he founded the Institute of Noetic Sciences, now based in Sausalito, California, which supports research and education on human consciousness.

Apollo 15 (July 26, 1971) pushed lunar frontiers out much further. While Alfred M. Worden circled in the command module, David R. Scott, commander, and James B. Irwin took the lunar module Falcon down into a treacherous landscape of canyons and mountains in the Apennius-Hadley region. The jagged peaks, rise to 12,000 feet (3657 meters) in height and resemble the American Rockies. Hadley Rille, a lunar Grand Canyon, cuts 1,200 feet (366 meters) deep and a mile wide. A miscalculation might have dashed the Falcon to pieces. In fact, the Falcon missed a crater rim by less than 15 yards (14 meters). It hit ground hard and pitched, but sustained no damage.

James B. Irwin, Apollo 15, stands by a Lunar Rover. Mount Hadley is in the background. David R. Scott, mission commander, took the photograph.

Scott and Irwin spent three days on the moon, making three EVAs in the Lunar Rover, the world's most expensive dune buggy. The development costs for the Rover had come to $38 million, double the estimate. NASA built only three, and all were left behind on the moon. The Rover was able to lumber along at about 10 miles (16 kilometers) per hour, and it enabled the astronauts to visit terrain miles from the lunar module.

Apollo 15's most significant find was the "genesis rock," so named because of its estimated age of nearly 4.5 billion years. It was found on August 1, after Irwin and Scott had driven to the base of the Apennine Front, stopping along the way to visit craters. At Spur Crater they found the rock, sitting on a pedestal-shaped boulder, almost beckoning to be picked up. In all, the team collected more than 170 pounds (77 kilograms) of surface material.

Another significant discovery was Scott's observation of "maybe ten well-defined layers" in the Hadley Rille canyon walls. This was the first eyewitness evidence that the lunar *maria* were not formed by meteor impact, or by a single volcanic eruption, but by a series of lava flows, perhaps over millions of years.

Since Shepard's golfing stunt, the crews that followed felt obliged to perform their own signature stunt. Scott tested Galileo's discovery that objects falling in a gravity field do so equally despite disparate weights. Scott dropped a hammer and a feather; both reached the moon's surface at the same time.

Irwin, a deeply religious man, also made international headlines and history by his comment, "I felt the presence of the Lord up there on the moon." He said he felt comfortable in that forbidding environment, a confidence bolstered by his sense of an ineffable, invisible and divine presence.

The crew of Apollo 16 (April 16, 1972), included Thomas K. Mattingly II, who stayed behind in the command module, and Charles M. Duke and John W. Young, commander, who landed the lunar module Orion at Descartes Highlands on the southeastern near face. They almost had to abort the mission; at 50,000 feet (15.24 kilometers), the engine control of the command module Casper went haywire, and Mattingly had to go on backup guidance.

Duke and Young stayed on the moon 71 hours, the longest yet, and made 3 excursions in the Lunar Rover, the last venturing out 12 miles (19 kilometers).

They collected 210 pounds (95 kilograms) of surface material.

Their most significant find was magnetic rocks with reversed polarity (some pointed up and others down). Previously, scientists had believed the moon had no magnetic field. The presence of magnetic rocks indicated the moon probably at one time had a molten core.

Duke and Young's "event" was a "Moon Olympics" before their television camera, in which Young attempted to set a record broad jump and Duke a record high jump. It nearly ended in

Apollo 16 commander John W. Duke leaps up in air as he salutes the flag.

disaster when Duke took his leap up in the air. His backpack went up over his head and he lost his balance. In the slow-motion of lunar gravity, he had time to contemplate the possibility of falling on his suit and splitting it wide open. When he hit ground and bounced, luckily the suit held. The only damage was a moment of embarrassment.

Apollo 17 (December 7, 1972), the last hurrah of human beings on the moon to date, made four firsts in lunar exploration history. It was the first to be launched at night, to carry a cargo of five live mice, to go to the easternmost sector of the moon and nearest the far side, and was the first American mission to carry a civilian scientist. The crew included Eugene A. Cernan, commander, Ronald E. Evans and Harrison H. "Jack" Schmitt, a civilian geologist. The mice were left in the cargo bay with radiation-sensitive filmstrips implanted in their scalps to collect data on the cosmic rays that bombard spacecraft (the mice were sacrificed upon return in the name of science).

Cernan and Schmitt landed in the lunar module Challenger on December 11 near the Taurus Mountains and the Littrow crater formation, a difficult site because of the proximity to the dark

Duke "Dreamed True"

Charles M. Duke, the lunar module pilot for Apollo 16, had a strange dream about a week before the mission lifted off in April 1972. He shared it only with John W. Young, the commander who would accompany him to the moon's surface.

In the dream, Duke and Young were driving the Lunar Rover up and across a ridge, when they came upon a set of tire tracks. Mission Control gave them permission to follow the tracks. After some distance, the men came upon a vehicle that looked just like the Rover, and two suited men in it who looked just like Duke and Young.

The dream sounds like seeing one's double—an exact replica of one's self—which in folklore is an omen of one's imminent death. Duke didn't take it that way, however. The dream was not a nightmare in tone, nor did it leave him feeling uneasy that he and Young might die on the moon. In the dream, they made it home, and he delivered part of the vehicle to NASA.

Duke's dream did come true in a way. On April 23, he and Young were driving the Rover on their third EVA; Duke had the rudder. Duke noticed that they were rolling up a crystalline black and gray hill identical to the one in the dream. He was momentarily distracted. Suddenly the Rover began to slide backwards down the slope, and Duke had to fight to keep it from overturning. When the Rover came to a stop, they saw the skid tracks ahead of them, as though another vehicle had been there before.

"Charley," said Young, "you said you were going to see some other tracks on the moon."

side of the moon. The men stayed for 75 hours and made 3 EVAs in their Rover and on foot, traveling more than 22 miles (35 kilometers) from base. During their second EVA, they made one of the most extraordinary finds of all the Apollo missions: orange soil. The Taurus-Littrow region yielded some of the oldest and some of the youngest rocks found by Apollo crews.

To close this momentous chapter in humankind's travels to the moon, Cernan left behind a plaque that read, "Here man completed his first explorations of the moon. May the spirit of peace in which we came be reflected in the lives of all mankind."

After Apollo

After Apollo 17, the culmination of the United States' $40 billion investment in reaching the moon ($24 billion for Apollo itself and $16 billion for Mercury and Gemini), space exploration funding was drastically cut. What was left was shifted to the short-lived Skylab, the Space Shuttle and other projects. Once the moon was conquered with Apollo 11, the public became apathetic to manned moon missions, despite their scientific importance. Turnouts for parades and celebrations upon the returns of subsequent crews were small.

When the Space Shuttle Columbia

exploded shortly after liftoff on January 28, 1986, killing all seven crew members, NASA's space program fell into disarray. Even though Space Shuttle flights resumed in 1989, the dream of flying the shuttle to an orbiting space

---

Seeing Colors on the Moon

When Apollo 12 astronaut Charles "Pete" Conrad, Jr., looked down on the surface of the moon in 1969, he commented, "The moon is a very light concrete color. In fact if I wanted to go out and look at something I thought was the same color as the moon, I'd go out and look at my driveway."

Despite the apparent drabness that Conrad noted, observers on earth and other Apollo astronauts have recorded a variety of colors on the lunar surface. In 1971, Apollo 15 astronaut James B. Irwin reported finding rocks that were white, black, green and "all conceivable colors," but the overall color effect of the moon was gray or brown.

Apollo 17 crew members Harrison H. "Jack" Schmitt and Eugene A. Cernan were riding in their Lunar Rover in an area known as the South Massif when they spotted a band of orange-colored material ringing a small crater. Schmitt surmised that the color was produced by a fumarole, a hole in a volcanic region from which gas is vented. In this case, Schmitt guessed, the gas was oxidized iron ore. From samples brought back to earth for laboratory analysis, the orange was later determined to be tiny colored glass beads. Scientists believe the beads had been formed billions of years

ago during volcanic activity. Nothing similar was found anywhere else on the moon.

In prior years, professional astronomers using large telescopes reported seeing brightly glowing colored spots and patches on the lunar surface. Mostly reddish, some bluish and purplish patches, and spots also have been seen.

These occurrences, known as transient lunar phenomena (TLP), are generally accepted as bona fide by scientists. Noted astronomer Patrick Moore compiled a list of over 700 TLP events, recorded from the start of serious telescopic observance of the moon through 1971.

Explanations vary, and none are definitive. Back when it was believed the moon had an atmosphere, the phenomena were described as lunar twilight. Since then, astronomers have speculated that TLP are caused by the release of gases from beneath the surface or by clouds of lunar dust being stirred upward.

By analyzing the dates of recorded TLP, one scientist concluded that the occurrences are most common when the moon is closest to the earth. That is when the planet's gravitational pull is the strongest and perhaps triggers the release of lunar gases.

station, a way station to the moon and beyond, seemed to be something for a distant, not immediate, future.

Many Americans feel they didn't get their $40 billion worth out of Apollo: the thrill of walking on the moon and the collection of 842 pounds (382 kilograms) of rocks didn't justify the cost. Yet the technological benefits of Apollo have had an ongoing ripple-effect, spreading into virtually every aspect of life. NASA counts more than 500 specific technology transfers, including products and processes that benefit science, industry, medicine and consumer goods.

One of the most significant benefits is the revolution in personal computers, made possible to a great extent by the incredible down-sizing and miniaturization achieved by scientists and engineers serving Apollo. In 1957, when the Russian Sputnik soared into space, an IBM master computer took up space

---

Memorable Quotes

"Whoopie! Man, that may have been a small step for Neil, but that's a long one for me."
> —Charles "Pete" Conrad, Jr.,
> Apollo 12, upon stepping onto
> the moon

"On the moon, all the stars circle around you every twenty-eight days instead of every twenty-four hours, and the sun moves around you the same way. Yet, the earth stays right in the same spot. I remember thinking if ancient man had been born on the moon instead of the earth, he would have had much more difficulty determining what was going on because things would have been in slow motion. But I felt pretty sure ancient cultures would have worshipped the earth and thought it was an eye because it would change from blue to white and you could see something moving up there that did look like a colored eye. No doubt they would think that was a god up there watching them. There's no telling the virgins they would have sacrificed to that thing."
> —Al Bean, Apollo 12

"As I stand out here in the wonders of the unknown at Hadley, I try to realize there is a fundamental truth to our nature. Man must explore. And this is exploration at its greatest."
> —David R. Scott,
> Apollo 15

"We is here, man! We is here!"
> —Eugene A. Cernan,
> Apollo 17,
> upon landing

"Okay, let's get this mother out of here!"
> —Eugene A. Cernan,
> Apollo 17,
> upon leaving the moon

Space Shuttles may someday take travelers part-way to the moon.

equal to a half-block of two-bedroom homes. During Apollo, the master computers at Mission Control were merely floor-sized, and were more powerful and faster. The on-board computers in the lunar module weighed only seventeen pounds (about eight kilograms). Incredibly, barely two decades later, the average desktop computer was far more powerful and faster than anything used for Apollo.

What potential does the moon hold for us in the future? Early hopes were pinned on finding valuable minerals on the surface or extracting water from the rocks. Both were dashed by the Apollo missions, which found neither. Another early plan called for establishing a military base on the moon. That, too, became obsolete. A lunar military base offers no strategic advantage in a day of chemical warfare, Star Wars and the proliferation of nuclear weapons and other "smart" arms.

Most likely, the moon would serve as an ideal site for astronomical research and a jump-off point for manned exploration of other planets, especially Mars, the planet of greatest interest. A lunar base and colony—perhaps established and maintained by a consortium of nations—could truly break new frontiers in humankind's knowledge of the

Lagrange Points

When two large celestial bodies orbit each other, a condition known as "Lagrange points" is created in the orbits. These are points where the gravitational and centrifugal forces acting on each body cancel each other out. The points are named after the French mathematician Joseph Louis Lagrange, who discovered them in 1772.

There are five Lagrange points in the earth's orbit around the sun, and five Lagrange points in the moon's orbit around the earth. The moon's Lagrange points are also affected by the gravitational pull of the sun.

The Lagrange points have great significance for space travel, for they are places where space stations and colonies could remain in stable orbits without fuel. Space stations between the earth and moon would be best located around the most stable Lagrange points, shown in the diagram.

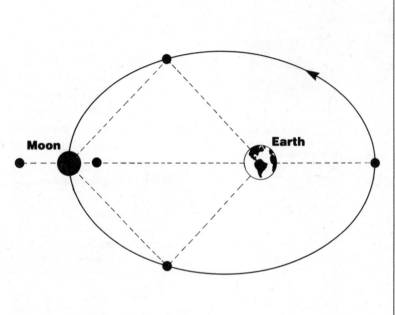

cosmos. Astronomers would rejoice at the moon's absence of atmosphere and the lack of interference from artificial lights and radio and other electromagnetic sources. Bulky observational equipment would be easy to move in the low gravity. And because the moon has a much slower rotation than the earth, it would be easier to take long-exposure photographs of the heavens. Spacecraft sent to explore other planets would have a much easier time leaving and returning to the moon due to the absence of atmosphere and the low gravity.

A lunar base might benefit earth as well. New researches and developments might be made possible, under the low-gravity conditions, in chemical, medical, surgical and technological fields.

The moon itself might make a colony self-supporting. The rocks brought back by Apollo crews were analyzed to

United States Postal Service stamps envision future mail delivery to the moon.

be 50 percent oxygen. If this oxygen could be extracted, or mined, it could be used to create potable water and liquid oxygen fuel for spacecraft.

In 1987, Sally K. Ride, the first American woman in space (on the Shuttle), wrote a report, "Leadership and America's Future in Space," which proposed establishing a space station and a moon base by the year 2001, and creating a permanent outpost by 2010, where up to thirty people could live for

a month to several months at a time. Key to this would be an operational lunar oxygen plant for the making of fuel and water. Ride envisioned the base's purpose as scientific and technological research.

Sadly, at the *fin de siecle*, both public and government interest in returning to the moon were at an all-time low due to pressing and worldwide economic, health and political problems. It was difficult to consider financing an expen-

---

Home, Sweet Home

Although it will be years—perhaps decades—before humankind attempts to colonize the moon, planners are already beginning to develop prototypes to house the first settlers.

Saudi Arabian architect Yousef Hijazi has proposed a prefabricated "self-erecting" structure modeled after those currently used as temporary shelter for pilgrims to Mecca.

Hijazi's four-story modular units—also envisioned as temporary housing until permanent structures could be built—would be packed into special cylinders for delivery to the moon. As soon as the spacecraft landed, these cylinders would roll off and the structures would unfold by themselves. Self-powered winches would lift each floor into place and then support columns and side panels would slide down from the ceilings. A solar-shield, to be filled with lunar soil, would surround the moon dwelling.

Japanese planners are working on de-

signs for moon houses fabricated from a type of concrete to be made from lunar soil. These "mooncrete" structures would be assembled by robots. The finished units would be covered with lunar dirt to shield people inside from meteors and cosmic rays. The only drawback: the absence of water on the moon to mix the "mooncrete." However, scientists say the concept could work if a source of hydrogen is located on the moon. Then the gas could be combined with oxygen extracted from moon rocks to create lunar water.

Some visionaries are even thinking ahead to the day when there will be hotels on the moon to house tourists. Others are exploring everything from creating an atmosphere on the moon that would support life to domed ecosystems that would resemble deserts, hot springs and woodlands.

One planner estimated it would cost $152 billion to build the first lunar colony.

sive lunar colonization program when funds were lacking to address serious problems on earth. In 1989, the twentieth anniversary of Apollo 11, humans on the moon seemed like an ancient memory and not the future's promise.

Nonetheless, a few optimists in the private sector planned for a coming time not only of a lunar base, but of lunar tourism as well. However, we may be well into the twenty-first century before these visions come to pass.

Lunar Missions

Unmanned flybys, orbits and landings

Date	Spacecraft	Description of Mission
10 Oct 1958	Pioneer 1 (USA)	flyby
6 Dec 1958	Pioneer 3 (USA)	flyby
1 Jan 1959	Luna 1 (USSR)	flyby
12 Sep 1959	Luna 2 (USSR)	crash-landed
Oct 1959	Luna 3 (USSR)	photographed dark side
Feb 1964	Ranger 6 (USA)	photographic/cameras malfunctioned
28 Jul 1964	Ranger 7 (USA)	photographic/crashed at Mare Nubium
17 Feb 1965	Ranger 8 (USA)	photos of Mare Tranquillitatis
31 Mar 1965	Ranger 9 (USA)	photos of Alphonsus Crater
May 1965	Luna 5 (USSR)	soft landing failed
18 Jul 1965	Zond 3 (USSR)	orbited and photographed far side
Oct 1965	Luna 7 (USSR)	soft landing failed
Dec 1965	Luna 8 (USSR)	soft landing failed
31 Jan 1966	Luna 9 (USSR)	successful soft landing/ photos of Oceanus Procellarum
31 Mar 1966	Luna 10 (USSR)	orbited/measured gamma-rays
30 May 1966	Surveyor 1 (USA)	color photos of Flamsteed
10 Aug 1966	LunarOrbiter (USA)	orbited/sent data and photos
24 Aug 1966	Luna 11 (USSR)	orbited
Sep 1966	Surveyor 2 (USA)	soft landing failed
22 Oct 1966	Luna 12 (USSR)	orbited/sent data
7 Nov 1966	LunarOrbiter 2 (USA)	orbited/sent photos

Lunar Missions, continued

21 Dec 1966	Luna 13 (USSR)	landed at Oceanus Procellarum/sent photos/ collected soil samples
4 Feb 1967	LunarOrbiter 3 (USA)	orbited/sent photos
17 Apr 1967	Surveyor 3 (USA)	landed at Oceanus Procellarum/ran soil tests
4 May 1967	LunarOrbiter 4 (USA)	orbited
14 Jul 1967	Surveyor 4 (USA)	lost contact with spacecraft
19 Jul 1967	Explorer 35 (USA)	orbited/measured magnetic fields
2 Aug 1967	LunarOrbiter 5 (USA)	orbited/sent data
8 Sep 1967	Surveyor 5 (USA)	landed at Mare Tranquillitatis/photos/soil tests
7 Nov 1967	Surveyor 6 (USA)	landed at Sinus Medii/photos
6 Jan 1968	Surveyor 7 (USA)	landed at Tycho Crater/ tested soil/sent photos
Apr 1968	Luna 14 (USSR)	orbited
14 Sep 1968	Zond 5 (USSR)	orbited
10 Nov 1968	Zond 6 (USSR)	flyby/photographic
13 Jul 1969	Luna 15 (USSR)	landed at Mare Crisium
Aug 1969	Zond 7 (USSR)	flyby/photos of western limb and far side
12 Sep 1970	Luna 16 (USSR)	landed at Mare Foecunditatis/brought soil samples home
Oct 1970	Zond 8 (USSR)	flyby/photographic
10 Nov 1970	Luna 17 (USSR)	landed at Sinus Iridum/soil tests
Sep 1971	Luna 18 (USSR)	soft landing failed
28 Sep 1971	Luna 19 (USSR)	orbited
Feb 1972	Luna 20 (USSR)	landed at Crisium basin rim/ obtained soil samples
8 Jan 1973	Luna 21 (USSR)	landed at Mare fill of Le Monnier/brought soil samples home
29 May 1974	Luna 22 (USSR)	orbited
Nov 1974	Luna 23 (USSR)	suffered damage on landing
9 Aug 1976	Luna 24 (USSR)	landed at Mare Crisium/ obtained soil samples

Apollo Manned USA orbits and landings

Date	Spacecraft	Crew	Description of Mission
11 Oct 1968	Apollo 7	Cunningham, Eisele, Shirra	Test orbits around earth
21 Dec 1968	Apollo 8	Anders, Borman, Lovell	First manned moon orbit
3 Mar 1969	Apollo 9	McDivit, Schweickart, Scott	Test orbit around earth
18 May 1969	Apollo 10	Cernan, Stafford, Young	Test orbits around earth
16 Jul 1969	Apollo 11	Aldrin, Armstrong, Collins	Landed at Mare Tranquillitatis/first men on moon
12 Nov 1969	Apollo 12	Bean, Conrad, Gordon	Landed at Oceanus Procellarum
11 Apr 1970	Apollo 13	Haise, Lovell, Swigert	Mission aborted
31 Jan 1971	Apollo 14	Shepard, Mitchell, Roosa	Landed at Fra Mauro
26 Jul 1971	Apollo 15	Scott, Irwin, Worden	Landed in Apennius-Hadley region/used Lunar Rover to explore surface.
16 Apr 1972	Apollo 16	Duke, Mattingly, Young	Landed at Descartes Highlands
7 Dec 1972	Apollo 17	Cernan, Evans, Schmitt	Landed at Taurus-Littrow

Selected Bibliography

Abel, E.L. *Moon Madness*. Greenwich, Conn.: Fawcett Publications, 1976.

Baker, Margaret. *Folklore and Customs of Rural England*. Newton Abbot, Devon: David & Charles, 1974.

Barrett, Francis. *The Mague*. London: Lackington, Allen and Co., 1801.

Briggs, Katherine. *British Folktales*. New York: Dorset Press, 1988. First published as *A Dictionary of British Folk-Tales* by Routledge & Kegan Paul, Ltd., London, in 1970–71.

Burl, Aubrey. *Rites of the Gods*. London: J.M. Dent & Sons Ltd., 1981.

Campbell, Joseph. *Myths to Live By*. New York: Bantam Books, 1988. First published 1972.

Corliss, William R. *The Moon and the Planets: A Catalog of Astronomical Anomalies*. Glen Arm, Md.: The Sourcebook Project, 1985.

Crawford, E.A. *The Lunar Garden: Planting by the Moon Phases*. New York: Weidenfeld & Nicholson, 1989.

Crossley-Holland, Kevin. *The Norse Myths*. London: Andre Deutsch Ltd., 1980.

Cunningham, Donna. *Moon Signs: The Key to Your Inner Life*. New York: Ballantine Books, 1988.

Eliade, Mircea. *Patterns in Comparative Religion*. New York: New American Library, 1958. London: Sheed & Ward, 1979.

Folklore, Myths and Legends of Britain. London: Reader's Digest Assoc. Ltd., 1977.

Givry, Emile Grillot de. *Witchcraft, Magic and Alchemy*. New York: Dover Publications, 1971. First published 1931.

Guiley, Rosemary Ellen. *The Encyclopedia of Witches and Witchcraft*. New York & Oxford: Facts On File, 1989.

Guiley, Rosemary Ellen. *Harper's Encyclopedia of Mystical and Paranormal Experience*. San Francisco: HarperSanFrancisco, 1991.

Guiley, Rosemary Ellen. *The Mystical Tarot*. New York: New American Library, 1991.

Guiley, Rosemary Ellen. *Vampires Among Us*. New York: Pocket Books, 1991.

Hamilton, Edith. *Mythology*. New York: New American Library/Mentor, 1942.

Harding, M. Esther. *Women's Mysteries Ancient and Modern*. New York: Harper & Row, 1971. London: Century Hutchinson, 1989.

Harley, Rev. Timothy. *Moon Lore*. London: Swann Sonnenschein, Le Bas & Lowrey, 1885.

Hawkins, Gerald S. *Stonehenge Decoded*. New York: Dorset Press, 1965.

Hultkrantz, Ake. *The Religions of the American Indians*. Berkeley: University of California Press, 1967.

Hurt, Harry III. *For All Mankind*. New York: The Atlantic Monthly Press, 1988.

Inwards, Richard (comp.) *Weather Lore*. London: Rider & Co., 1950.

Katzeff, Paul. *Full Moons*. Secaucus, N.J.: Citadel Press, 1981.

Lewis, Richard S. *Appointment on the Moon*. Rev. ed. New York: Ballantine Books, 1969.

Lieber, Arnold L. *The Lunar Effect: Biological Tides and Human Emotions*. Garden City, N.Y.: Anchor Press/Doubleday, 1978.

Mayo, Gretchen Will. *Star Tales: North American Stories About the Stars*. New York: Walker & Co., 1987.

Mercatante, Anthony S. *Encyclopedia of World Mythology and Legend*. Frenchs Forest, Australia: Child & Associates, 1988. New York: Facts On File, 1988.

Monaghan, Patricia. *The Book of Goddesses and Heroines*. St. Paul: Llewellyn Publications, 1990. First published by E.P. Dutton, New York, 1981.

Moore, Patrick. *Guide to the Moon*. Guildford and London: Lutterworth Press, 1976.

Opie, Iona and Moira Tatem (eds.). *A Dictionary of Superstitions*. Oxford: Oxford University Press, 1989.

Otten, Charlotte F. (ed.) *A Lycanthropy Reader: Werewolves in Western Culture*. New York: Dorset Press, 1989. First published 1986.

Paulsen, Kathryn. *The Complete Book of Magic and Witchcraft*. Rev. ed. New York: New American Library, Signet, 1980.

Piggott, Stuart. *The Druids*. London: Thames and Hudson, 1975.

Price, Fred W. *The Moon Observer's Handbook*. Cambridge: Cambridge University Press, 1988.

Proctor, Mary. *Legends of the Sun and Moon*. London: George G. Harrup & Co., Ltd., 1926.

Randolph, Vance. *Ozark Magic and Folkore*. New York: Dover Publications, 1964. First published 1947.

Swainson, Rev. C. *A Handbook of Weather Folk-lore*. Edinburgh & London: William Blackwood & Sons, 1923.

The Helen Oxenbury Nursery Rhyme Book. Rhymes chosen by Brian Alderson. New York: William Morrow, 1986. First published by William Heinneman Ltd., London, 1986.

Thomas, Keith. *Religion and the Decline of Magic*. New York: Charles Scribner's Sons, 1971.

Trigg, Elwood B. *Gypsy Demons & Divinities*. Secaucus, N.J.: Citadel Press, 1973.

Tyler, Hamilton A. *Pueblo Gods and Myths*. Norman, Okla.: University of Oklahoma Press, 1964.

Waite, A.E. *The Book of Black Magic and of Facts*. York Beach, Me.: Samuel Weiser, 1972. Hastings, East Sussex, England: Society of Metaphysicians, 1986.

Werner, E.T. Chalmers. *Myths and Legends of China*. London, 1922. Reprint. New York: Benjamin Blom, 1971.

Wilkins, H.P. and Patrick Moore. *The Moon*. London: Faber and Faber Ltd., 1968.

Williamson, Ray A. *The Living Sky: The Cosmos of the American Indian*. Norman, Okla.: University of Oklahoma Press, 1984.

Yeats, W.B. *Irish Fairy and Folk Tales*. New York: Dorset Press, 1986. Also published as *Fairy and Folk Tales of Ireland*. Gerrands Cross, Buckinghamshire, England: Colin Smythe, 1988.

Photo and Illustration Credits

David Anstey: 7, 8 (bottom), 17, 18, 20, 21, 22, 25, 26, 27, 29, 95, 113, 185; author's collection: 11, 12, 19; Al George: 4, 5; NASA: 10, 14, 46, 165, 167, 168, 169, 171, 172, 173, 174, 178, 180, 184; Reading Rainbow Gazette, Inc.: 151; Caroline Smith: 45, 92, 126, 131, 144; U.S. Games Systems, Inc., Rider Waite Tarot deck: 138, 139; U.S. Postal Service: 161, 186

Index

Alchemy, 76–77
Apogee, 8–9, 41
Astrology, 127–35
Aubrey, Sir John, 93
Beer, Wilhelm, 35–36
Blue moons, 38–9
Buddha, 45, 61, 90
Calendars, 9, 38, 75, 84, 86–95, 115
Copernicus, Nicolaus, 7, 34
Craters, 8, 10–12, 22–23, 175–80
Dracula, 150, 158–60
Eddy, John, 94–96
Fairies, 156–57
Galilei, Galileo, 7–8, 34–35, 179
Halo, 22, 108
Harvest moon, 9, 89, 126
Hawkins, Gerald, 93–94
Herschel, Sir John, 32, 36–38
Herschel, Sir William, 30, 32, 35
Hevelius, Johan, 8, 34
Hewelcke, John, 8, 34
Jung, Carl G., 131–32
Lagrange, Joseph Louis, 185
Lagrange, points, 185
Librations, 19–21
Limb, 17, 29–30, 41
Lunar dust, 15–16, 22
Lunar eclipses, 23–29, 42, 109
Lunar phases, 17–19, 24, 38, 75, 97, 99,
  101, 105–11, 113, 118, 122–24, 126–
  27, 132, 144
Lunar rocks, 15–16, 34, 172, 174–75,
  180–81, 183, 185–86
Lunar soil, 15, 34, 172, 174–75, 186, 188
Mädler, Johann Heinrick, 35–36
Man in the moon, 50–54, 75
Mare, 8–11, 16–17, 170, 179, 187–88
Medical astrology, 111–14
Medicine wheels, 94–96

Moon: age of the, 16, 179; atmosphere of
  the, 9–10, 13, 15, 17, 22–23, 30–34,
  40, 185; far side of the, 17, 19, 180;
  and fertility, 75–77, 83, 85, 89, 99–
  100, 106, 108; gods and goddesses of
  the, 6, 75, 79–86, 89–91, 97, 115–16,
  120, 122, 145; and harvesting, 99–100,
  105–06; life on the, 31–34, 36–38,
  175, 186; and madness, 6, 141–60; and
  magic, 6, 115–40; maps of the, 8, 34,
  36; orbit of, 8–9, 15, 19–20, 24–25,
  30, 40–42; origin of the, 13, 15, 44;
  and planting, 6, 99, 101–03, 105–06;
  revolution of the, 9, 19; rotation of the,
  9, 17, 19–20, 42, 185; size of the, 7, 9,
  40; symbols of the, 27, 29, 76–78, 83–
  84, 91, 121; temperature on the, 16–17,
  34, 40; and weather, 108–11
Moonbow, 22, 108
Moonquakes, 13, 16, 22
Moon signs, 129, 130
Myths, 6, 43–74
National Aeronautices and Space
  Administration (NASA), 92, 164, 166–
  67, 173, 175–77, 179, 182
Native Americans, 43, 47–52, 54, 56, 59,
  65–66, 70–71, 76, 79, 83, 88–89, 94–
  96, 148, 152
Nodes, 24–26, 40–42
Occultations, 29–31
Pachrates, 115, 122
Palmistry, 6, 135–38
Perigee, 8–9, 42
Pickering, William Henry, 36
Pliny the Elder, 96, 100
Plutarch, 31, 83
Ptolemy, 7, 131
Rays, 11–13
Riccioli, Giambattista, 8, 34

Rilles, 10–11, 42
Saros cycle, 26, 42
Schroeter, Johann Hieronymous, 35
Schroeters, M., 33
Sidereal month (or period), 9, 40, 42
Solar eclipses, 24–26, 28–29, 42
Stonehenge, 91–94
Synodic period, 40, 42
Tarot, 6, 138–40
Terminator, 17, 42
Tides, 13, 16, 20–21, 75, 99, 103, 115,
  148
Transient lunar phenomena (TLPs), 13, 183
Soviet space program: Luna, 17, 162–63,
  187–88; Sputnik, 162, 188; Zond,
  187–88
U.S. space program: Apollo, 8, 11, 13,
  15–16, 34, 164–85, 187, 189;
  Explorer, 162, 188; Gemini, 164, 166,
  181; Lunar Orbiter, 187, 188; Mariner,
  12; Mercury, 164, 166, 181; Orbiter,
  164; Pioneer, 162, 187; Ranger, 162–
  63, 187; Saturn, 166–67, 175; Skylab,
  181–82, 184, 186; Surveyor, 12, 164,
  175–76, 187–88; Viking, 12
Vampires, 6, 27–28, 149–50
Von Gruithuisen, Franz, 22, 32
Waning moon, 17, 19, 99–100, 105–07,
  109–10, 112–13, 115, 118, 121–22,
  127, 132
Waxing moon, 17, 19, 99–100, 105–07,
  109–10, 112–13, 115, 118, 120–26,
  132
Werewolves, 6, 141, 151–56
Witchcraft, 96–98, 116, 120, 122, 142
Woman in the moon, 54, 56–59
Yin and Yang, 45, 63
Zodiac signs, 112–14, 118, 128–30,
  132–35